BEYOND THE FIVE-PARAGRAPH ESSAY

BEYOND THE FIVE-PARAGRAPH ESSAY

KIMBERLY HILL CAMPBELL & KRISTI LATIMER

STENHOUSE PUBLISHERS
PORTLAND, MAINE

Stenhouse Publishers
www.stenhouse.com

Credits
Page 127: "The Queen's Complaint" from *The Collected Poems of Sylvia Plath*, edited by Ted Hughes. Copyright ©1960, 65, 71, 81 by the Estate of Sylvia Plath. Editorial material copyright ©1981 by Ted Hughes. Reprinted by permission of HarperCollins Publishers.

Library of Congress Cataloging-in-Publication Data
Campbell, Kimberly Hill.
  Beyond the five-paragraph essay / Kimberly Hill Campbell and Kristi Latimer.
     p. cm.
  Includes bibliographical references and index.
  ISBN 978-1-57110-852-4 (pbk. : alk. paper) -- ISBN 978-1-57110-956-9 (ebook)
  1. English language--Composition and exercises--Study and teaching (Secondary) 2. Exposition (Rhetoric)--Study and teaching (Secondary) 3. Essay--Authorship. I. Latimer, Kristi. II. Title.
  LB1631.C36 2012
  808'.0420712--dc23
                                                                          2011044233

Cover design and interior design by Blue Design (www.bluedes.com)
Manufactured in the United States of America

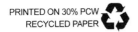
PRINTED ON 30% PCW
RECYCLED PAPER

18 17 16 15 14 13   9 8 7 6 5 4 3 2

CONTENTS

ACKNOWLEDGMENTS

We want to acknowledge the graduate students who inspired the conversation that led to the creation of this book. We realized if we were going to challenge the five-paragraph formula, we needed to research and provide alternatives to it. Kimberly teaches language arts methods courses to graduate students, and Kristi works with these same students in a summer course titled Writing in Response to Literature. We want to recognize the contributions the students in these classes have made to this book. They asked questions that pushed our thinking and reported what they were seeing and wondering about with respect to their work as student teachers in a variety of middle school and high school classrooms.

We are also grateful to the amazing teachers we know and work with who were so gracious about sharing their teaching stories and strategies with us. We are honored to include the work of these talented colleague collaborators: Marisa Real, Tatiana Lawson, Kara McPhillips, Gabrielle Buvinger-Wild, Rob Vaughn, Ben Klash, Colin Pierce, Lori Townzen, Jennifer Wecker, Dylan Hardy, Mollie Dickson, Kara Wendel, Carrie Strecker, Erin Ocon, Joe Dessert, Rachel Pass, Sharon Klin, Nicola Onis, and Edward Derby. Each of you informs and inspires us.

We want to express our gratitude to the middle school and high school students who have been in our classrooms, sharing their ideas, asking questions, challenging our assumptions—and our work with them. They remind us that we need to continue to be learners as we teach. It is our hope that this book reflects the lessons they have taught us about how to create language arts classrooms that support and nurture writers and thinkers.

Our editor, Bill Varner, and the team at Stenhouse Publishers supported us each step of the way, from the proposal to publication. Thank you.

We also want to acknowledge Jim Whitney, who is the master behind the photos in the book and on the back cover. It is our pleasure to work with you, Jim.

As the References and Suggested Works sections of the book illustrate, we are grateful to so many writers, scholars, and teacher-researchers to whom we turned for information, clarification, and/or inspiration.

Each of us is fortunate to have a support network that made the writing of this book possible. Kimberly is grateful to the following wonderful folks:

Kristi Latimer, a coauthor who asked good questions and met deadlines—even when pregnant—and whose commitment to teaching secondary and graduate students is truly remarkable.

Ruth Shagoury, for her listening ear during the creation, writing, and revising of the book.

My colleagues at Lewis & Clark College Graduate School of Education and Counseling, who provided support and encouragement.

My parents, Gil and Vonnie Hill, who taught me that I must finish what I start, even when it does not feel doable.

My son, John, who provided technology support during the writing of the book, as well as graphic novel, film, and TV references—and Kevin Smith's eulogy.

My daughter, Kinsey, who provided literature examples, checked reference citations, shared stories from her high school and college literature classrooms—good and bad—and was always up for a Starbucks run.

My patient and supportive husband, Michael, who moved boxes of books and piles of folders on and off the dining room table (also known as my office), tolerated late-night and weekend writing sessions that interfered with family life—and meals—and did not flinch at the money spent ordering books in support of this book.

Kristi's support network includes the following wonderful friends and family:

Kimberly Campbell, coauthor and researcher extraordinaire, who first taught me so much about teaching, and then, eight years later, guided me through the process of learning to write a book.

My colleagues at Tigard High School, especially Lori Townzen, Jodi Mello, Joe Dessert, and Frank Caro, whose resourcefulness and creativity inspire me to be a better teacher.

My mom, Sandy Latimer, who always believes in me, and, with loving memory, my father, Roy Latimer, whose humor and humility prepared me well for teaching.

My son, Guy, whose birth derailed this book for a few months, but whose delight in all things keeps my days filled with joy.

My daughter, Vera, who graciously sacrificed mommy-time while I wrote, and who showed her support for my work by covering her board books with multicolored tabs.

My husband, Dylan, whose combination of irreverence for traditional instruction and inspired teaching pushes his students—and me—to both marvel at and challenge the world around us.

CHAPTER 1

COMBATING FORMULAIC WRITING

The stack of essays I hauled home on Friday sits on my desk, waiting to be read. It is now Sunday afternoon. As I grab my third cup of coffee and read the first essay, I groan. And groan. Essay after essay demonstrates that my students have mastered the five-paragraph formula. I can easily find the thesis at the end of the first paragraph. There are three supporting paragraphs with some quotes from the text. And the conclusion paragraph restates the thesis. Organization is evident but thinking is not. From conversations with my colleague Kristi, I know this reflects her experience when reading and responding to essays. Although we were comforted in knowing we shared this perennial frustration, we reached out to our other colleagues in search of an answer. How could we move students beyond the five-paragraph formula? How could we change the focus of essays about literature to developing an argument and defending it? Over and over again we heard and empathized with the challenges we face as language arts teachers: large class sizes, students with complex and diverse learning needs, and the pressure to prepare students to pass standardized tests, which may require formulaic responses. We also discussed the realities of classroom practice, where students often resist reading longer texts and are quick to latch on to the five-paragraph formula in writing about literature they may or may not have read.

In these conversations, the resistance of both colleagues and students surprised us when we pondered a different approach to writing about literature. Their defense of the five-paragraph essay was fierce. Over and over we heard about the critical importance of organization. We heard about how the formula was essential for students who were developing their analytical writing skills. We heard about how the formula was required to do well on standardized tests. Graduate students were vehement that the formula got them ready for college. And we heard from a number of teachers about how the use of the formula provided an objective standard that supported fair evaluation. Support for the five-paragraph formula was strong, if not compelling.

So we looked to the research and were stunned to find that research does not support literary essays taught in a five-paragraph formula: a thesis at the end of the first paragraph, followed by three paragraphs with examples from the text, and a conclusion that restates the thesis. While we did find articles touting the benefits of the formula, we noted that they were typically "opinion" pieces rather than research studies. And the number of both opinion and research articles challenging the five-paragraph formula was staggering. As high school English teacher and department chair Kimberly Wesley notes, "Teachers of the five paragraph theme . . . have become complacent in their acceptance of a tool that purports to nurture but, in fact, stunts the growth of human minds" (2000, 57).

How did this happen? Why would so many of us teach an approach to writing about literature that did not serve our students well?

Textbook publishers and the standardized testing establishment play a role in promoting the formula. But the five-paragraph formula exists because we, as language arts teachers, accept the myths that support it.

Members of the UNC Charlotte Writing Project challenge us to rethink our reliance on the formula:

> Our concern is for *what* the five-paragraph essay teaches students and with *what* the five-paragraph essay does not teach them; our concern is with what students learn to do by writing in this format and with what students will not learn because of the continued presence of this mythic form. Our concern is for the students who are subjected to this form and spend their intellectual lives constrained by its insistence. (Brannon et al. 2008, 17)

THE MYTHS OF THE FIVE-PARAGRAPH FORMULA

Thirty years of research confirm the failure of the five-paragraph formula. (For examples of this research, see the archived occasional papers and technical reports of the National Center for the Study of Writing and Literacy 2011, which are housed on the Web site of the National Writing Project: http://www.nwp.org/cs/public/print/doc/resources/techreports.csp.)

We have summarized this research in the following discussion of the myths that have been offered in defense of the five-paragraph formula. It is our hope that as middle school and high school teachers of writing we will dispel these myths and focus our attention on writing practices that serve our students well.

Myth: The five-paragraph formula is an actual form.
Both of us have been hard-pressed to find essays written in the five-paragraph formula beyond the school walls. But within school walls it is pervasive; we have even seen posters in support of the formula: an inverted triangle representing an introduction paragraph that starts broad and narrows to a thesis, followed by three rectangles, representing three supporting paragraphs, and a final triangle, to show how the conclusion restates the thesis and builds out from it. And we have heard English teachers speak to the importance of the five-paragraph form. These teachers

> speak a logic that is important to challenge precisely because this logic
> perpetuates the commonsense myth that the five-paragraph theme is an
> actual "form" and that "forming" in writing is simply slotting information
> into prefabricated formulas rather than a complex process of meaning-
> making and negotiation between a writer's purposes and audiences' needs.
> (Brannon et al. 2008, 16)

In an effort to make writing more accessible, the formulaic approach "forces premature closure on complicated interpretive issues and stifles ongoing exploration" (Wiley 2000, 61).

Myth: The formula is just a starting point; it's a necessary first step that supports students in moving to more sophisticated writing.
The problem with this myth is that the focus of writing instruction becomes the formula, not the content of the essay. Teachers can efficiently focus on thesis statements followed by five-sentence supporting paragraphs and a conclusion that restates the thesis. But studies indicate that most students never move beyond this formula. "The FPT [five-paragraph theme] formula may assist students with proper formatting of papers, but it appears to fall short of helping them offer a *cogent discussion of their thoughts*. Worse, strict adherence to the FPT may actually limit students' development of complex thinking" (Argys 2008, 99).

Kristi met with resistance from students when she began moving the seniors in her International Baccalaureate (IB) class beyond the five-paragraph formula. They had been successful with this formula in high school and did not want to let it go. Their comments also demonstrate that they had not been given the opportunity to think beyond the formula: "So I don't have to have three sentences of analysis per quotation? Then how do I know I have a complete paragraph?" Another ranted, "I don't even know how to write this now. My whole structure is shot." And several students lamented, "Why have we been taught to do this for so many years?"

And Kristi's IB students are not alone in their frustration with the five-paragraph formula. Jennifer Courtney's (2008) study of first-year writing students at a large southeastern university found that students felt constrained by the five-paragraph formula. Rather than seeing it as a support for more sophisticated writing, they saw it as the definition of academic writing. In interviews, students reported that academic writing had to be a certain length (five paragraphs) and follow the rules.

Imposing an arbitrary format makes learning to write just that much harder, and for no good reason, like learning to play tennis in leg chains (Brannon et al. 2008, citing Knoblauch and Brannon 1984).

Myth: The formula is a helpful tool for students who struggle with writing.
"When students are considered lacking—lacking organization, lacking ideas to write about, lacking understanding—writing in an arbitrary formula merely sustains the deficit perception" (Brannon et al. 2008, 18). When asked to use the five-paragraph formula, students learn that writing is about sentence placement, not about discovery and ideas.

In her study of English language learners in a college remedial writing course, Elizabeth Rorschach was surprised to discover the negative impact of the five-paragraph formula. She writes, "I had initially set out to examine the three students' sense of audience as they revised but found myself sidetracked by what actually impelled their revisions. Their choices as writers were based on satisfying structural requirements . . . These students ended up producing essays that were disjointed, disconnected, unexplored, and weak, with minimal revision between drafts, and yet the essays received praise and high grades from teachers who seemed to value only adherence to form" (2004, 17). The student example provided by Rorschach to illustrate her concerns follows the five-paragraph formula.

Struggling writers need support in developing their ideas and finding structures that allow their ideas to be understood by a reader. "[B]ut repetitively following the same direction for writing every essay will not help these writers advance beyond a kind of 'successful' codependence on teachers who have agreed in advance that this sort of formulaic essay will be what they reward" (Wiley 2000, 65).

All students should have the opportunity to discover that their ideas matter and are worthy of exploration and shaping to meet the needs of readers—not a formula.

Myth: The formula prepares students for standardized tests.

"I cannot tell you when it happened that the process became a formula resulting in five-paragraph themes, but I believe it was the scoring rubric of the standardized test and pressure to teach our students how to be successful based on that rubric that resulted in formulaic writing," admits Glenda Moss, former Texas middle school teacher (2002, 24). Moss's experience in Texas is not isolated. Standardized testing has led to more writing in schools, but at "the expense of actual writing instruction and experience" (Fanetti, Bushrow, and DeWeese 2010, 78, citing Fisher and Frey 2003). Although the prevalence of the five-paragraph formula can be linked to the increase of standardized writing assessments, studies indicate that the formula does not lead to high test scores. For example, a study of the Delaware student testing program found that essays with no organization earned low scores; essays that followed the five-paragraph theme (FPT) earned middle range scores (score of 6 on a 2–10 scale), but every essay that earned a high score (8 or better) "used other than the FPT organizational scheme" (Albertson 2007).

A 2003 report presented by the National Commission on Writing in America's Schools and Colleges also points to a lack of elaboration among students' standardized essays.

With regard to the SAT, which has been under scrutiny for its usefulness as a measure of student aptitude or predictor of college success (Adelman 1999, Ballinger 2008), the writing portion of the test has increased the criticism of the test's usefulness. In 2005, Sarah Lawrence College joined a growing list of schools that no longer require the SAT. The dean of admissions found the SAT writing tests, while well intentioned, would "not be helpful" in assessing applicants for a "writing-based curriculum such as ours." The SAT twenty-five-minute writing requirement is "not at all reflective of how our students are going to have to write many lengthy papers based on long-term research, analysis, and discussion" (Gross 2003, 1).

The five-paragraph formula has not proved useful for students entering colleges that consider the SAT writing exam. According to *Newsweek* magazine, SAT essay evaluators do not favor the five-paragraph formula. "In the scoring we saw, students who wrote formulaic five-paragraph essays didn't get the highest scores." Ed Hardin, a College Board content specialist, notes that formulaic essays "can lack coherence and a progression of ideas" (Setoodeh 2005, 9). This is consistent with research on standardized writing at middle and high school levels (Albertson 2007; Brannon et al. 2008; Fanetti et al. 2010).

Glenda Moss (2002) grew so frustrated with the test-preparation focus of her teaching in Texas that she resigned. She notes:

Increasingly, I have come to understand the long-range negative effect on our students when the five-paragraph theme is the only standard. I now regret that I spent more time helping them to write to pass the TAAS than I did helping my students to make the connection between writing skills as tools to express their thoughts, values, and beliefs. (25)

Myth: The formula prepares students for college writing.

College professor Elizabeth Rorschach notes that when she reads the five-paragraph formula her students rely on, "I find myself terribly disappointed by how shallow and un-thought-out most of the five-paragraph essays are" (2004, 17). And she is not alone. Numerous studies and articles have been written about college professors' frustration with the limitations of the five-paragraph formula (Fanetti, Bushrow, and DeWeese 2010; Kidwell 2005; Moghtader, Cotch, and Hague 2001; Moss 2002; Smith 2005). Even college students recognize the formula's limitations. In a survey of first-year college composition students, the recommendation was that their high school teachers quit "driving the 5-paragraph thing into our brains" (Randsell and Glau 1996, 19).

As discussed, Jennifer Courtney's study of first-year college writing students found students were frustrated with the formula because it did not allow them or prepare them to deviate from the formula (2008).

Trinh Nguyen tells her story of unlearning the five-paragraph essay to be successful in college writing. "Do not write a five paragraph essay. Not all paragraphs have to be the same size. Topic sentences don't always have to be at the beginning of each paragraph." These were the professor's opening remarks in Trinh's first college writing class. She was shocked to learn that the five-paragraph formula she had mastered in high school was no longer useful (Smith 2005, 1, citing Nguyen).

Writing instructors of first-year composition courses at a large metropolitan university "routinely describe having to spend the first half of their semester unteaching the skills and traits students acquired during high school, encouraging initiative, autonomy, and invention" (Fanetti, Bushrow, and DeWeese 2010).

Myth: Teaching the five-paragraph formula is teaching writing.

Donald Murray drew on his own years of experience as a writer in asserting that the five-paragraph formula "had little to do with the exciting, mucking-about process of real writers" (Romano 2000, 74).

A dissertation study of high school students and academic writing confirms Murray's assertion in finding that the fill-in-the-blank structure of the five-paragraph essay "did not allow students to do what real writers do, develop compositional goals, make plans to reach those goals, and address rhetorical and pragmatic concerns that develop during composing, or to practice making strategic decisions as writers must do" (Kane 2005, 194–195, quoted in Argys 2008, 98).

College professor Rorschach criticizes the "view of writing that this shortcut engenders. The preset formula lulls students into nonthinking automaticity. It causes a closing down of the natural human tendency to draw connections and see patterns and relationships in our experiences" (2004, 19).

Middle school teacher Lesley Roessing revamped her writing program when she realized that the five-paragraph essay was not teaching her students to be writers. She notes:

> **As I read about style and voice, I realized that I had been caught up in listening to others instead of to my heart, trying to fulfill what I thought were the expectations of the students' future teachers rather than listening to the voices of the students. I had taught personal style right out of my students. It was time to put the writer back in the writing. (2004, 42)**

*   *   *

As we read the research critiquing the five-paragraph formula, we began to examine our own practice and process for writing in response to literature. We realized we came at the development of thesis statements in different ways. In response to some literature, our thesis statements came at the end of the essay. (For more discussion on thesis development, see Chapter 6.) We realized we sometimes had more than three supporting paragraphs with textual evidence, and sometimes we had only two. We both expressed our struggle to write conclusions that do more than restate the thesis. We want conclusions to show that our essays really do have something important to say. We acknowledged that essay writing requires time; it is messy—even frustrating. But we have also experienced the joy of discovering what we know through writing. We understand the power a well-crafted essay can have to push and challenge our thinking. We know that essays that do not follow formulas exist in the world beyond school, because they help readers examine and understand the world. There are essays that demonstrate what Susan Orlean, editor of the 2005 edition of *The Best American Essays*, looked for in her selection of essays, "an awareness of craft and forcefulness of thought" (2005, xiii). This is what we want our students to understand as they write essays about literature.

BEYOND THE FIVE-PARAGRAPH FORMULA

Moving beyond the five-paragraph formula is an opportunity for us to rethink the role of literature and writing in our middle school and high school classrooms.

> **To coax our students to let go of the five-paragraph essay, we're going to have to be convinced ourselves that the goal of the English class is not to read a certain number of books and write a certain number of essays about them. We need to believe that English class is a bustling crossroads of human condition, a portal to places and experiences around the world and across time and, simultaneously, "a room of one's own," a place where each student has mental and emotional space to engage in personally meaningful work. (Miller 2010, 100)**

We need to change how we structure our classrooms and how we support students as writers. We need to create classrooms where reading literature and writing about literature are both seen as "acts of construction and expression" (Fischer 2000, 41). This process will not be easy, and we have discovered it can be messy, and even frustrating, for teachers and students. When we move from asking students to follow a formula to developing an essay based on what they think about the literature they have read, we put the emphasis on thinking—deep thinking. We want students to articulate this thinking and support it with evidence from the text. We want their writing to show their thinking. What we are calling for in this approach is a reclaiming of the literary essay!

The remaining chapters of this book provide details on how to create classrooms that educate and encourage essays about literature that we, as teachers, want to read.

Chapter 2: Establishing a Routine of Thoughtful Reading and Writing

In Chapter 2 we introduce the foundation for a literature workshop, where the active work of reading and writing in response to literature happens in class. We describe the key components of this workshop and share strategies that stimulate student thinking, value unique insight, and encourage writing that is lively, personal, and well organized.

Chapter 3: Reading Like a Writer

In this chapter we share strategies that encourage students to read as writers— "lingering over every word, every phrase, every image, considering how it enhanced and contributed to the story as a whole" (Prose 2006, 13). This close reading is the foundation for writing about literature.

Chapter 4: Writing and Discussion in Support of Thinking

As Purves, Rogers, and Soter describe, "Writing, unlike other avenues for response, offers an opportunity to explore what we think and to record that exploration simultaneously" (1995, 151). Chapter 4 explores the use of a variety of strategies and low-stakes writing options that support students in thinking as they read. This writing can then be used by students in the development of exploratory, analytical, and creative responses to literature (see Chapters 5, 6, and 7).

Chapter 5: Writing to Explore

This chapter explores writing about literature to discover, to explore, to consider possibilities. Students will build on the skills and strategies they have developed as close readers and in low-stakes writing to support their thinking. They will provide examples and quotes from the text in support of their explorations. But their explorations may lead to a series of notes about a text, an appreciation for multiple perspectives, or even uncertainty, which leads to new questions. We share our discoveries about the power of collaboration in support of discussion, debate, and writing as well as organizational structures that support writing as exploration.

Chapter 6: Writing as an Authority

At the heart of good essay writing, like all writing, is support for content development. Students need to know what they are trying to say. Throughout Chapter 6 we stress the importance of writing process—focusing on students as they write. We discuss strategies, mini-lessons, and a continued focus on writing process in support of analytical essays—essays in which students take a stand and defend it. Our goal is for students to discover and demonstrate their voice as literature authorities.

Chapter 7: Writing with Mentors

In this chapter we explore writing in the form of the literature students are reading and analyzing: a poem to reflect on a poem, a character sketch based on the reading of a short story with rich character development, an essay that draws on the structure of essays students have studied. This takes the notion that we read literature as a model for good writing and makes the modeling explicit. Students are asked to step into the structure and voice of an author's work—to try it on. Tom Romano writes, "Imitation of an author's ways with words can create a gush of language. Imitation can cut loose a voice and let writers experience the power that comes with a little recklessness, a little letting go of the self and learning the language rhythms and voice habits of another" (2004, 101).

CHAPTER 2

ESTABLISHING A ROUTINE OF THOUGHTFUL READING AND WRITING

We picture a classroom where adolescents are engaged in reading, discussing, and understanding literature—a wide range of literature. We picture a classroom where writing about literature is a regular in-class routine. Rather than see writing about literature as a task to complete, an assignment to endure, or a test to pass, we want students to see writing about literature as a way to capture their thinking about literature. As Linda Rief notes:

> Writing is not about memorizing a series of facts and reiterating that information on a multiple-choice test or within the response of a contrived essay question, only to forget it all the moment the test is over. Writing lets us think of things we didn't know until we began writing. Writing is one way of representing and communicating our thinking to others, using our experiences, our knowledge, our opinions, and our feelings to inform and negotiate our understandings and misunderstandings of ourselves and the world in which we live. (2007, 191)

This view of writing as support for thinking informs the way we approach writing about literature. The emphasis is on generating ideas and then exploring those ideas, turning them over, asking questions, considering other viewpoints. The goal is not to come up with an idea about a literature text and follow a formula to explain the idea. The goal is for students to use writing in support of their thinking about a text: to comprehend what the text is saying, to personally connect with the text, to identify issues, to interpret what the text means, to examine the author's craft, to compare and contrast the text with other texts, to consider why the text matters, to reflect on their own strategies and processes as readers and writers.

This exploration of writing in support of thinking is supported by a classroom where reading and writing happen in a community of learners, a classroom where collaboration is encouraged, where the teacher shares his or her own processes as a reader and writer, where skills are modeled and practiced in support of reading and writing, where ongoing assessment is used to inform instruction, and where feedback on students' writing is timely, targeted to specific objectives, and includes students' self-assessment and reflection.

LITERATURE WORKSHOP

In support of this classroom, we propose an approach to literature instruction that draws on the research and classroom practice of workshop proponents (Atwell 1998; Blau 2003; Kittle 2008; Rief 1992; Romano 1987). In a literature workshop format, students are engaged in reading and writing about literature during each class period. Blau notes that the focus of a literature workshop is as "much on the *process* of reading and producing discourse about literature as it is on the *substance* of discourse produced" (2003, 13; emphasis added). Students in a literature workshop are engaged in the exploration of "genuine questions or problems" that require them to develop skills in literary study and discourse while thinking about and reflecting on their own process of encountering the question or problem (2003, 13). Rather than be the "expert-teller" of what the literature means, the teacher is a fellow participant.

This does not mean our role as teachers is diminished in the literature workshop. Quite the contrary, we draw on our expertise in selecting texts, framing questions or problems to explore, identifying the skills and strategies students will need to develop or refine, developing classroom structures and lessons that will support students' explorations, and designing and modeling formative and summative assessments in which students demonstrate their knowledge and understanding.

Students are given choice, time, and models of good writing to support their learning (Rief 2007). A variety of low-stakes writing opportunities (Elbow 1997), with support through teacher modeling and mini-lessons, will lead to final-draft responses to literature that include essays and more. (See Chapters 5, 6, and 7.)

Choice

We propose the incorporation of choice about what literature is read in literature workshop. We are not suggesting that the teacher abdicate control over literature selections, but we do recommend that teachers provide opportunities for choice about what literature students read some of the time. In support of choice, we have asked students to vote on a selected text from a list of options. For example, in a junior English class, students voted on a list of Edgar Allan Poe stories, selecting "The Black Cat" as their first choice. In an eighth-grade classroom, students were given the following list of short-story titles along with a brief description of each story:

"The Lottery" by Shirley Jackson
"Marigolds" by Eugenia Collier
"Everyday Use" by Alice Walker
"Harrison Bergeron" by Kurt Vonnegut
"Checkouts" by Cynthia Rylant

The students selected "The Lottery," which they found surprising, even creepy. They then asked if they could read the rest of the stories on the list (an unexpected but delightful surprise). Lists of texts in support of choice can be generated based on author or genre, or by having students select from the table of contents in a required literature anthology.

Literature circles also support choice and allow students to work with peers to read and explore a text. Students in a junior English class read Emily Dickinson's poem "This Is My Letter to the World" as a class. After this whole-class exploration, students formed literature circles based on their choice of another Dickinson poem. They built on the whole-class exploration of her poem by reading, discussing, and analyzing their poem choice. Each group then took on the role of expert in presenting their group's poem to the class. Picture a music video of "Because I Could Not Stop for Death." (For more on literature circles, see Daniels 2002 and Daniels and Steineke 2004.) Text sets of short literature selections allow students to all read the same genre yet choose their own titles from within the selections provided. We have used text sets in support of essay and memoir reading. We compile file folders with essays or memoir excerpts arranged by topic or theme. Students are instructed to read a select number or a variety of topics and themes. (For more on text sets, see Tovani 2004, 43–48.)

Choice is also an option for writing about literature. We recognize the value of working with a community of learners on one kind of written response, but we also know the power of choice (Atwell 1998; Rief 1992, 2007; Romano 1987; Spandel 2005) and suggest that there is room for this kind of choice in literature response. (See more discussion in support of student choice in literature response in Chapters 5, 6, and 7.)

Time
We know that students learn to write by writing. And we know this means we need to provide time in class for writing (Atwell 1998; Rief 1992, 2007; Spandel 2005).

But with all of the curriculum mandates, we often spend more time talking about literature—often with the talk dominated by teachers—rather than providing time for students to write about literature.

In-class writing time should include exploration of ideas through low-stakes writing, modeling of how to develop ideas in support of literature exploration, attention to revision, and opportunities to reflect on one's writing process as well as on finished products.

Writing is complex, and we want students to explore this complexity while they are in the process of writing. Our hope is that students will develop a "repertory of routines, skills, strategies, and practices, for generating, revising, and editing different kinds of texts" (NCTE 2004, 2). We also want to stress the importance of reflecting on writing process—not as a formula or set of steps to follow, but as an ongoing exploration of what writing processes work best for individual students and in different writing situations.

We are also interested in fostering habits of writing that go beyond the classroom. It's our hope that students will see that writing has multiple purposes and formats. We want students to use writing for personal growth and reflection, for exploration, as a form of creative expression, to demonstrate understanding, for varied audiences, and as a way to participate in society (NCTE 2004). Chapter 7 discusses ways to use time in class to explore writing that goes beyond the classroom through the use of literature mentors, a variety of literature responses, and opportunities to share writing.

In support of writing about literature, we recognize the importance of time in class for talking. This includes discussions about literature that encourage a variety of voices, not just ours as teachers. Although classroom talk is not the focus of this text, we will share ways to use writing in support of literary discussion and provide resources that we find useful in support of classroom discussion. We also recognize the importance of time spent talking about writing that is in process. This includes conferences with peers and teachers, particularly in the early stages of writing when ideas are being explored (see Chapter 4). And, we value the role of oral presentations in the development of literate language and practices (see Chapter 4).

Models

There are two issues with regard to modeling. First, students need to read and study examples of the writing we are asking them to do. This means reading poetry in support of writing poetry and reading essays about literature in support of writing essays about literature. We know the challenge of finding models to share with students. We will share how we have worked to address this challenge, including resources for published models and using students' work to model literature response.

Second, we need to model the writing we are asking our students to do (Graham and Perin 2007; Rief 2007; Spandel 2005). As Donald Murray notes, "An interesting way to become a writing teacher who writes is to write your own assignments" (2007, 181). We recognize what we are asking by this recommendation; we are adding more work to already overworked language arts teachers. But it has been our experience that the benefits of doing the literature assignments we ask our students to do far outweigh the extra time and effort it requires:

- We can provide a model of what an assignment might look like.
- We can share our process with students, which includes actively modeling and teaching revision and editing.
- We can make changes in the assignment based on our experiences in trying to do the assignment; in some cases this means radical revision or even dumping an assignment.
- We can determine mini-lessons we need to teach to help students meet the learning objectives.
- We can be seen by our students as fellow learners. This changes their relationship with us. Our feedback on their work is informed by our own experience with the work. The Siletz Indians have a wonderful quote that captures this relationship: "One who learns from one who is learning, drinks from a running stream."
- This modeling, through examples and by us, as teachers, is consistent with differentiated instruction research (Tomlinson 1999).

Knowing Our Students Well

Another important aspect of the literature workshop is knowing our students well. In a recent interview, a high school senior complained about her English class, reporting, "My English teacher doesn't know anything about me, and it's clear she doesn't want to know anything about me." For this student, the lack of relationship—or any interest in a relationship—leaves her feeling disconnected and disinterested in the work of the class. Tomlinson and McTighe (2006) address the need to build strong teacher-student relationships in support of student learning, noting, "Beyond the potent benefits of human beings learning to understand and appreciate one another, positive teacher-student relationships are a segue to student motivation to learn. A learner's conviction that he or she is valued by a teacher becomes a potent invitation to take the risk implicit in learning" (18). We also take to heart the work Kathleen Cushman (2003) and her colleague Laura Rogers (Cushman and Rogers 2008) have done in interviewing high school and middle school students about their advice for teachers. Both groups want to be known by their teachers. The strategies we list in Figures 2.1 and 2.2 for getting to know students in the literature workshop are consistent with the students' advice. We encourage you to check out Cushman, Rogers, and the students' work (see References).

Figure 2.1

STRATEGY: INTRODUCTION LETTERS (SEE APPENDIX A1 FOR AN EXAMPLE.)
Compose an introduction letter to students with information about who you are as a reader and writer. Suggest questions that students can respond to in writing their own introduction letters to you. Provide class time for students to draft their letters. We also recommend providing stationery for students to use for their letters.
IDEAS FOR MODIFYING THIS STRATEGY Provide in-class time for partner introductions. Use this in addition to letter writing or in lieu of letter writing. Use a postcard format instead of a letter format.
ASSESSMENT AND FEEDBACK Circulate as students are writing to answer questions and read over their shoulders; encourage them to "say more" when needed. Write a letter back to each individual student. We know the time commitment this involves but have seen the impact of individual responses. (Stationery that is smaller than notebook paper or postcards work well to limit the amount written but still provide an individual response.) An alternative to an individual letter in response to each student is a letter to the class that captures patterns you discovered while reading their letters. We strongly recommend that you handwrite one or two sentences to each individual student at the bottom of this general letter. Another alternative is to write responses in the margins and return the letter. But we have found it helpful to keep a copy of each student's letter as a writing sample and to refer to these letters as planning for the year unfolds.
ADDITIONAL DATA-GATHERING STRATEGIES (SEE APPENDIX A2, "STUDENT SURVEY FOR THE FIRST WEEK OF SCHOOL") Survey students' experiences with literature and writing. Gather data regarding students' daily schedules, including after-school obligations.

Figure 2.2

STRATEGY: READING TIME LINE
Have students create a time line of their reading history. We've found that using grade levels or favorite books as the focus of the time line works well.   Provide 11-by-14-inch paper and colored markers for students to create their time lines.
IDEAS FOR MODIFYING THIS STRATEGY   Ask students to share the story of a favorite book they've read.   Ask students to respond to the prompt: I remember reading _____.   Ask students to bring in a favorite book and to share an excerpt from it with the class.
ASSESSMENT AND FEEDBACK   Use these stories of reading as an opportunity to respond to individual students and to generate shared stories of reading. We use sticky notes to make comments about students' time lines, focusing on connections we share with the students' reading histories as well as previewing ways they might connect with texts we will be reading.

Selecting Literature

As noted previously, we do support student choice regarding literature selection. But we are still proponents of a literature workshop in which the whole class sometimes reads the same text. We have witnessed the discoveries that come from exploring a shared text as a community of readers and writers.

The relationships we build with students support our efforts in selecting literature. But how do we decide on shared texts? Probst calls for literature selection based on "its potential to interest students" (2004, 67). This is simple advice but it is often overlooked in our efforts to teach the curriculum—or what's in the bookroom. Probst reminds us that our focus must be on our students and what is appropriate for them. He notes that the texts we select "must not be too difficult or easy—syntactically or conceptually" (67). This can be difficult to judge and is further complicated by the diversity of students in our classrooms and the unique skills each one of them brings to the work of reading and writing about literature. And we are well aware of requirements based on department and district expectations. But we have discovered that taking time to read a text we plan to teach through the eyes of our students is worthy work. We look at the vocabulary of the text, places where students may need background information to support comprehension, and opportunities for students to make connections to previous texts they've read, their own lives, and issues in the world. This process allows us to see the book with new eyes and to develop reading and writing activities that will support students' exploration and analysis of literature.

Literature Responses

The literature workshop reflects our commitment to a response-based approach to literature that supports students as readers and writers. Our aim is to "affect students' perceptions of works of art (literary works), to affect their ability to articulate their responses, to affect their tolerance of the diversity of human responses to similar objects, and to bring them together in a community of communities" (Purves, Rogers, and Soter 1995, 69). In an effort to meet this aim, students will need to read, think, and write about literature in a variety of ways (responses). Drawing on the research of Blau 2003; Probst 2004; Louise Rosenblatt 1978, 1995; and Scholes 1982, 1985, we have created the following categories of literature responses—recognizing that these categories overlap:

KINDS OF RESPONSES

- Comprehension: What does the text say?
- Personal: What connections can I make to the text based on my experience?
- Interpretive: What might the text mean?
- Form/Craft: How did the author accomplish the effect of the text?
- Text to Text: How does this text compare/contrast with other texts?
- Authoritative: What is my stance and what evidence do I have from the text in support of my argument?
- Critical: Why does the text matter?
- Inspirational: How can I use the text as a mentor for my own writing?
- Habits of Mind: What strategies do I use to read and understand this text?

In designing our literature workshop, we draw on this list of responses in thinking about the literature we choose, the strategies and skills students will need to read the text, and the kinds of writing—low stakes and high stakes (Elbow 1997)—students will generate. We also think about timing: What writing will students do before they read, while they read, and after they have read? And as mentioned previously, we continually stop and look at our instructional decisions through the eyes of our students.

PLANNING A LITERATURE WORKSHOP UNIT

Planning is the foundation of the literature workshop, so we wanted to share how we think about planning and the resources we draw on in support of our efforts. Backward design (Wiggins and McTighe 2005) supports our literature workshop efforts. As Wiggins and McTighe suggest, we use essential and unit questions to frame the big picture of reading and writing. We then use the three focus questions of backward design as a basis for unit and yearlong plans:

1. *What do we want students to know, understand, and be able to do?*
2. *How will we know what students know, understand, and are able to do?*
3. *What teaching and coaching will be needed in support of students' knowing, understanding, and doing?*

We briefly describe the backward design approach to planning in the following sections. To learn more about backward design, see Wiggins and McTighe (1998, 2005).

Essential and Unit Questions

We relish the early stages of planning for literature workshop, because the possibilities seem limitless. It's wonderful to make a list of all the reasons for teaching a text using the kinds of literature responses listed on page 20. But then our task is to consider our students and what it is we want them to take from this literature exploration. We find that asking ourselves what we want them to remember at the end of the unit, at the end of the year, and in five years is helpful in identifying the big ideas, or what Wiggins and McTighe call "enduring understanding," which they define as follows:

> **Represents a big idea having enduring value beyond the classroom**
> **Resides at the heart of the discipline (involves "doing" the subject)**
> **Requires uncoverage (of abstract or often misunderstood ideas)**
> **Offers potential for engaging students (1998, 23)**

In our own classrooms, we want students to understand that we read and write about literature to know ourselves, others, and the world.

Essential questions help us frame what we want students to understand. "To get at matters of deep and enduring understanding, we need to use provocative and multilayered questions that reveal the richness and complexities of a subject" (Wiggins and McTighe 1998, 28). We use essential questions to frame a quarter, semester, or even the entire school year:

> **How does American literature define and reflect what it means to be American?**
> **What is the American Dream and has it changed over time?**
> **Why do we share stories?**
> **What does it mean to be a hero? How does literature explore the ideal of hero?**

How do we find our voice through writing?

What is community? What role does narrative play in forming/supporting community?

What is a great book?

In addition to big-picture essential questions, we have found it helpful to use unit questions to frame literature workshop studies. "Unit questions are more subject- and topic-specific, and therefore better suited for framing particular content and inquiry leading to the more subtle essential questions" (Wiggins and McTighe 1998, 30).

How did Emily Dickinson and Walt Whitman change American poetry?

What does *Death of a Salesman* say about the American Dream?

What are the elements of a short story?

Is Odysseus a hero?

What is nonfiction, and why do we read and write it?

What does "home" mean?

Posting the essential and unit questions and referring to them throughout the literature study provides a framework for students' thinking.

Planning Questions

From essential and unit questions, we move to planning questions. These questions support the development of objectives and assessment, which then allow us to craft activities in support of these objectives and assessments. We confess that we have both been guilty of focusing first on activities, without linking the activities to objectives or assessment. We now find we are spending more time planning, but the reward is that we see how this planning supports students' learning. As noted previously, we consider Wiggins and McTighe's (2005) three questions in developing our plans:

1. What do we want students to know, understand, and be able to do?
We look to district, state, and the IRA/NCTE (1996) standards in identifying objectives for our students. Kristi also works with IB students, so she uses IB guidelines. Drawing on these various standards that frame our work, we have developed the following objectives for literature workshop:

Students will develop and demonstrate a variety of reading strategies in support of comprehending literature.

Students will reflect on their habits as a reader in support of comprehending literature.

Students will use close reading strategies in support of literary analysis.

Students will use low-stakes writing as a way to explore and capture their thinking about literature.

Students will develop written and oral discussion skills that enable them to converse with others about the literature they read.

Students will explore and demonstrate a variety of written and oral responses to literature.

Students will explore writing process in crafting drafts of essays in response to literature.

Students will know and use peer response protocols in support of their writing efforts.

Students will recognize the role of literature in their lives.

Students will recognize the role literature plays in helping them understand the experience and culture of others.

2. How will we know what students know, understand, and are able to do?

We use a variety of assessments in response to this question. And we think about and carefully plan the timing of assessments. We want to check in with students before we start a unit (preassessment), during the unit (ongoing assessment), and at the end of the unit, when students demonstrate understanding (summative assessment). The big change in our thinking comes from having to consider these three types of assessment at the beginning of a unit.

We readily acknowledge that we revise our unit plans as we teach, including assessments. But we have found that going into a unit with a summative assessment in mind focuses our teaching.

Examples of summative assessments can be found in Chapters 5, 6, and 7. In Chapters 3 and 4 we provide examples of assessments that could be used as preassessments and/or ongoing assessments.

3. What teaching and coaching will be needed in support of students' knowing, understanding, and doing?

Responding to this question is where activities become the focus. With regard to literature, we find it helpful to think about what we want students to do before they read the text, as they read the text, and once they have read the text.

And we would be remiss if we did not note the importance of considering accommodations we will need to make to support the diverse students in our classroom. We appreciate how the literature workshop approach supports differentiated instruction both through time in class to do the work and through choice regarding process and product. We describe teaching strategies in figures throughout the book as well as alternatives that can be used as accommodations for students with differentiated learning needs. (See the "Sample Unit Plan" in Appendix A3.)

CHAPTER 3

READING LIKE A WRITER

We know the soothing quiet of a classroom where students are immersed in reading. We know how much we all want to believe that students are thinking and making connections as they read. But we have learned the hard way that too often we have unintentionally set students up for frustration and even encouraged fake reading.

Our classroom practice has changed because we understand our job is to *teach* students how to respond to a text, and much of that instruction must happen during reading and not after. We cannot expect students to craft a meaningful and honest essay in response to a text if we do not help them find meaning *as they read*. Given the wide range of summaries and analyses available to students through online sources, such as CliffsNotes, it is easy for them to avoid actual reading. We must scaffold their reading process, helping them know what to look for, such as characters, setting, theme, and writing craft. In this chapter we discuss methods we have discovered for actively teaching students prereading and during-reading strategies that will help them question and analyze the text from the moment they open the cover. In Chapter 4, we discuss the use of low-stakes writing in support of thinking about the texts they are reading. We recognize that reading and writing happen in tandem in the classroom. We hope our organizational decision to address this in two chapters supports your planning and teaching of writing in response to literature.

DEVELOPING RESPONSES AS THEY READ

As noted in Chapter 2, we plan backward; we start by identifying what we want students to know, understand, and be able to do in response to the text we are teaching. This includes being clear about the focus of responses and clear about the final product students will create when they finish reading. Will they be writing an exploratory essay or question paper (Chapter 5), an analytical essay (Chapter 6), or a response to literature that uses the genre of the literature as a mentor (Chapter 7)? We make this decision before we begin reading the text so that the reading and writing strategies we teach from the time they begin reading will support the final assessment. We want students to be thinking about what they want to explore or analyze in their writing throughout their reading of the text. We have learned that teaching students strategies to focus on the author's structure and craft *during* the reading of a text is more effective in supporting students' understanding of the text than reading quizzes, which are often punishments for neglecting homework rather than valid measures of a student's independent thought and engagement. And reading quizzes are not helpful when it comes time to write about the text.

We recognize that if we want students to craft literature responses that demonstrate deep thinking about a text, we, as teachers, must teach and model reading strategies that enable deep thinking. We are well aware of the number of students, particularly high school students, who have mastered their skills as "fake readers" (Tovani 2000). Our antidote to "fake reading" is an emphasis on strategy, "an intentional plan that readers use to help themselves make sense of their reading" (Tovani 2000, 5). We use these strategies to support students' understanding and to push students to develop their thinking beyond just basic comprehension of the text.

In support of reading strategies that nurture students' thinking and writing in response to literature, we revisit the "Kinds of Responses" we discussed in Chapter 2. These responses support reading strategies as well as the writing in response to literature we discuss in Chapters 4–7.

KINDS OF RESPONSES
- Comprehension: What does the text say?
- Personal: What connections can I make to the text based on my experience?
- Interpretive: What might the text mean?
- Form/Craft: How did the author accomplish the effect of the text?
- Text to Text: How does this text compare/contrast with other texts?
- Authoritative: What is my stance, and what evidence do I have from the text in support of my argument?
- Critical: Why does the text matter?
- Inspirational: How can I use the text as a mentor for my own writing?
- Habits of Mind: What strategies do I use to read and understand this text?

We also want to revisit here the importance of choosing texts, because we have learned that the choice of texts we ask students to read, analyze, and write about can impact their success.

CHOICE OF LITERATURE
We have read stunning student essays about longer texts that have challenged students

as readers and writers. And we embrace the challenge of supporting students in this effort.

But we have also discovered that shorter texts can be the way into analytical essay writing for many students: short stories, poems, essays, and children's books. Heather Lattimer's wonderful text, *Thinking Through Genre: Units of Study in Reading and Writing Workshops, 4–12*, has a great chapter (Chapter 7) on writing in response to literature, with a compelling essay written by an eighth grader about the delightful children's book *The True Story of the Three Little Pigs!* by Jon Scieszka (Lattimer 2003, 266–267). Children's books are accessible and often deal with important topics that support analytical essay writing. Other children's book titles that have worked well for student essays are the following:

The Lorax **by Dr. Seuss (story of ecological issues)**

Letting Swift River Go **by Jane Yolen (story of the government purchase and flooding of a town to create the Quabbin Reservoir in Massachusetts)**

Sitti's Secret **by Naomi Shihab Nye (story of an American child who writes to the president of the United States on behalf of her Palestinian grandmother)**

For more examples of children's books that could be used to support writing in response to literature, see Chapter 7 in Kimberly Campbell's *Less Is More: Teaching Literature with Short Texts, Grades 6–12*.

We also want to recommend the use of young adult (YA) novels in support of writing about literature. Throughout this book, we stress the importance of students having something important to say and strategies that support this thinking. Interest in the topic of their essay is the foundation for good writing. We have witnessed heated debates about the characters of Edward and Jacob in the Twilight series. Kimberly listened to a debate between her English-major sister and her majoring-in-English daughter regarding which Twilight character was the better choice of boyfriend. Their use of textual evidence in support of each character was impressive. And the opportunity to explore the female main character in this series, Bella, is rich with possibilities. The Hunger Games series also lends itself to analytical exploration. A colleague reported a conversation she overhead: A group of sophomore girls were debating the portrayal of the female leads in Twilight and The Hunger Games. Again, text examples framed the heated debate. The powerful novel *Speak* by Laurie Halse Anderson has inspired students to explore the role of voice, the use of metaphor, symbolism, mascots, the "lies" told about high school, and the issues of sexual assault and depression and why students need to read texts that deal with these issues. As Hipple (2000) notes,

> Those less familiar with young adult literature tend sometimes to believe that its thematic treatments are slight or superficial—"teenage," if you will. They are not. Like the best of literature written for adults, good novels written for adolescents possess themes that merit and reward examination and commentary. (2)

And we want to tout the use of graphic novels as texts to read and analyze in and of themselves as well as in support of reading and understanding other texts. We have seen students embrace the opportunity to read a graphic novel as literature. In Portland, Oregon, area high schools, the graphic novel *Persepolis* by Marjane Satrapi (2003) is grabbing the attention and interest of students. This compelling autobiography of a young girl growing up in Iran during the Islamic revolution comes to life with words and simple black-and-white graphics. *Maus I: A Survivor's Tale: My Father Bleeds History* by Art Spiegelman (1986) is more than a tale of surviving the Holocaust; it also addresses the story of survivors and the impact on their families. We have seen this graphic novel taught at the middle and high school level.

Graphic novels can also support students' reading. We have used a graphic novel collection of Ray Bradbury short stories (Bradbury 2003b). And we recommend the following graphic novel adaptations: *Ray Bradbury's Fahrenheit 451: The Authorized Adaptation* by Ray Bradbury and Tim Hamilton, *Graphic Classics: Mark Twain*, *Graphic Classics: Edgar Allan Poe*, *The Odyssey* by Homer and Ray Thomas, *Romeo and Juliet* by William Shakespeare and John McDonald, and *Pride and Prejudice* by Jane Austen and Nancy Butler.

Teaching Texts That Are Not Our Choice

We would be remiss if we did not acknowledge that sometimes we are required to teach a text that would not be our choice. In this situation, we have found it helpful to find out more about the required text. Why this text? Is it the author? The time period? The writing craft? Or perhaps it is the beloved favorite of a fellow department member. Asking for the rationale for requiring the text can lead to a conversation about whether other texts are options. We have had success with using a short story by an author in lieu of that author's novel. For example, we have used the story "Winter Dreams" by F. Scott Fitzgerald in lieu of *The Great Gatsby* and "A Wagner Matinee" by Willa Cather rather than *My Antonia*. (See Campbell 2007, page 69, for more examples.) We have been able to use literature circles for a greater variety of texts that represent a particular time period or theme. But we have also taught required texts we would not choose to teach. While we do not recommend sharing this view with students, we do support using reading strategies that emphasize select sections or chapters in the text and summarizing other chapters. We will also admit to discovering the possibilities of a text by teaching it.

Whatever our "choice" of text, we need to find ways to invite our students into the text.

INVITING STUDENTS INTO LITERATURE

> *Literature is unique as a discipline . . . a literary work is inevitably dormant until it is read. True, the text is there, but the ink on the paper amounts to little until a reader picks up the page, reads, and responds to it and thereby transforms it into an event. It is the experience that the text invites and enables the reader to have that makes it literature.*
>
> —Robert E. Probst (2004)

Our challenge is to create a classroom space where students can discover the possibilities literature offers. In the sections that follow, we discuss strategies that support students in accepting the "invitation" to delve into a text.

Tapping into Students' Background Knowledge

Ellin Keene reminds us that we need to support students' understanding throughout their reading experience, which includes "the use of 'way-in' texts—picture books and short pieces of texts students can use to build background knowledge (schema) and provide a way in to understanding more abstract, concept-and-vocabulary-laden texts" (2007, 29). We have used music and photographs from the 1920s to set the stage for *The Great Gatsby* by F. Scott Fitzgerald. Children's books can be good entry points. We recommend reading *Edgar Allan Poe's Tales of Mystery and Madness* before reading Poe's short stories and poetry and *Henry David's House* before reading *Walden* by Henry David Thoreau. *A Brilliant Streak: The Making of Mark Twain* by Kathryn Lansky provides insight into Twain's life experiences and writing. And *Emily Dickinson's Letters to the World* by Jeanette Winter serves as a great introduction to an exploration of Dickinson's poetry. (Note: The children's books listed on page 29 could also be used in support of background knowledge.) Even episodes of *The Simpsons* can be used (see further discussion on page 40 in this chapter).

Quick-write prompts encourage students to explore topics related to the literature we are going to read. "What do you remember about your first day of high school?" or "How would you describe your high school to a new student?" are prompts students can write about before reading Laurie Halse Anderson's novel *Speak* or Sherman Alexie's novel *The Absolutely True Diary of a Part-Time Indian*.

We have also used anticipation guides to encourage students to begin thinking about issues or themes that will be raised in the text. (See Appendix B1, "Sample Anticipation Guides.")

In the following sections, we discuss reading strategies that also serve to support students' understanding of literature before and as they read.

First Impressions

It's tempting to jump into an explanation of why the text students are going to read is important. But this doesn't allow students to discover the text on their own. And it doesn't allow for the development of habits that will support and sustain students in making choices as readers throughout their lifetime. We drew on our own bookstore habits in crafting strategies to support choice reading—and discovered we can adapt these strategies when reading an assigned text in literature workshop.

We notice titles when exploring books in a store. There are several ways to scaffold students' exploration of the text's title. An exploration of each word in the title works well. We have done this by handing cards with individual title words to students and asking them to write out all the possible definitions they know. We then put the cards together to form a series of titles, with student definitions. Titles that work well for this exploration include the novels *Of Mice and Men* by John Steinbeck, *Catcher in the Rye* by J. D. Salinger, *Heart of Darkness* by Joseph Conrad, and *I Know Why the Caged Bird Sings* by Maya Angelou, and the short stories "The Mark on the Wall" by Virginia Woolf, "The Life You Save May Be Your Own" by Flannery O'Connor, and "Letter from the Fringe" by Joan Bauer.

We also find it useful to invite students to do a quick write in response to the title, as described in Figure 3.1.

Figure 3.1

STRATEGY: EXPLORING THE TITLE
Write the title on the board or overhead.
Ask students to do a quick write based on their response to the title, using these prompts:
Have you heard of the title? If so, what do you know about it?
What does the title suggest the book might be about?
Can you think of books with similar titles?
What connections do you see between the title of the text and our essential question(s)?
IDEAS FOR MODIFYING THIS STRATEGY
Have students work in pairs or groups to discuss the title.
Provide one question (from list above) to each student.
ASSESSMENT AND FEEDBACK
Ask students to share their quick writes with the class or in small groups.
Collect quick writes and skim them, identifying familiarity with title and other patterns.
Return quick writes after students have done some reading and ask them to reflect on what the title means now.
Revisit the meaning/impact of individual words in the title as reading continues.

Judging a Book by Its Cover

Building on the title exploration, we hand out the text and spend some time looking at what we can learn from the front and back covers.

Marisa Real, who teaches in a high school on the Oregon coast, finds it useful to use a graphic organizer in support of cover exploration. Her teaching strategy is described in Figure 3.2 and in the paragraphs that follow.

After students have completed the "First Impressions" graphic organizer and have read the opening chapter of the text, Marisa invites them to use the "Second Impressions" graphic organizer—or, "Judging a Book by What's Between the Covers"—to reflect on what they now know based on the lead (see Appendix B3). For more on leads, see page 36.

Figure 3.2

STRATEGY: FIRST IMPRESSIONS
Hand out the "First Impressions" graphic organizer (see Appendix B2).   Ask students to list things they notice based on the front and back cover of the book they're about to read. Students then revisit their lists and note what they think about the things they noticed.   Synthesis: Have students reread their lists and thoughts about the lists and jot down a few statements about the book based on their analysis of the front and back covers.
IDEAS FOR MODIFYING THIS STRATEGY   Model your own list of things you notice about the back cover and have students focus on the front cover.   Have students work in pairs or groups to examine the front and back covers.
ASSESSMENT AND FEEDBACK   Ask students to share their initial lists and synthesis.   Post students' synthesis statements.   Collect students' "First Impressions" graphic organizers and assess them based on completion and/or note patterns in students' responses to support future discussion.

We have discovered that there are a number of texts that have multiple versions with different front and back covers. This strategy can be adapted by having students meet in small groups to compare and contrast their thoughts about the different covers, using the graphic organizers to support their conversation. It is helpful if you have copies of the texts with the different covers, but if not, provide pictures of the different covers. Listed here are a few of the texts with different covers that we have explored with students:

The Awakening by **Kate Chopin**
Their Eyes Were Watching God by **Zora Neale Hurston**
To Kill a Mockingbird by **Harper Lee**
The Grapes of Wrath by **John Steinbeck**
A Separate Peace by **John Knowles**
The Great Gatsby by **F. Scott Fitzgerald**
The Woman Warrior by **Maxine Hong Kingston**
I Know Why the Caged Bird Sings by **Maya Angelou**

Meet the Characters

Asking students to take on the role of the characters in a text before they have read the text is another way to invite students in. We are grateful to our colleague Linda Christensen (2000) for the idea of the literary tea party. Her strategy is described in Figure 3.3.

Figure 3.3

STRATEGY: CHARACTER TEA PARTY
Hand out a character statement to each student. (See Appendix B4, "Character Tea Party," for examples.)
Have students list thoughts or questions about their character after reading the character statement and determine what information they want to share during the tea party.
Provide students with a separate character sheet on which other characters are listed. (See Appendix B4.)
Have students then take on the role of their character and mingle. Either during or just after the tea party, they should jot down what they have learned about the characters listed on the character sheet.
IDEAS FOR MODIFYING THIS STRATEGY
Model a character role-play and have students take notes.
Provide students with character role sheets that require them to meet three or four characters rather than all the characters.
Allow students to role-play their characters in small tea-party groups rather than as a whole class.
ASSESSMENT AND FEEDBACK
Ask students to write about each character they met and how they are related to the other characters.
Invite students to draw the character they played and/or the characters they met or "cast" the part of each character. What real actor would play this character and why?
Have students make predictions about the characters and/or the book.

Please note we recommend the inclusion of iced tea, lemonade, or another beverage, and light snacks to create a tea-party atmosphere. We do want to share that although the setup for this strategy can be labor intensive, we have noticed that students often develop an affinity for the character they portray and stay focused on this character as they read. In Appendix B4 we have included teacher Tatiana Lawson's tea-party character statements for the book *The Breadwinner* by Deborah Ellis. Tatiana used this story, set in Afghanistan, with sixth-grade students in a humanities class that linked literature with world geography. We have also included in Appendix B5 a variation on the character tea party, a "Launch Party" for *The Great Gatsby*, created by teachers Kara McPhillips and Gabrielle Buvinger-Wild. In their "Launch Party," photos of the actors in the new film version of *The Great Gatsby* (2012) were included in the character section—for example, Leonardo DiCaprio is pictured for Jay Gatsby. Unfortunately, due to copyright costs for the actor photos, we could not include them in the example. (See the section titled "Reading with an Eye on Literary Structure," beginning on page 46, for more on character exploration.)

Reading Aloud

We concur with Appleman's call for reading texts aloud: "There is no better way to hook kids than to read to them the first chapter of a book" (Appleman 2007, 146). We use reading aloud to model the close reading of leads or the entire opening chapter, and we support reading aloud beyond the first chapter. Janet Allen reminds us of the value of reading aloud as students follow along in the text. She notes students' positive feedback on the effectiveness of being read to by the teacher in their end-of-year surveys. Allen also provides her own insights regarding the impact of shared reading in noting how this technique

> allowed me to model reading strategies I employed when I came to
> unknown words, concepts, or inconsiderate sentences; show excitement as
> well as sadness in my appreciation of the characters' lives and problems;
> encourage discussions in which everyone could participate; extend the
> story to our lives and build community background knowledge; and
> demonstrate ways in which readers question themselves, the text, and the
> author in order to make the experience personally meaningful. (1995, 63)

The Lead

Both of us appreciate a good lead, both in texts we read and in the writing our students do. So we relish the opportunity to use literature as a model for good leads. We want students to read and reread the opening of a book or short text and really focus on what they notice. As we note in the section titled "Judging a Book by Its Cover," we appreciate how Marisa Real invites students to think about their "Second Impressions" after reading the lead or opening chapter (see page 34). A second strategy for examining leads is described in Figure 3.4.

Figure 3.4

STRATEGY: WHAT I KNOW SO FAR/WHAT I WANT TO KNOW
Hand out a copy of the lead or ask students to follow along in the text as you read the lead aloud.
Pose the following question: What do we know so far? Students should jot down their response in a quick write.
Ask students to reread the lead with the following questions in mind:
Who is telling the story?
What do we know about the setting?
What do we know so far regarding what is happening?
What do you predict will happen next? What did you hear that suggests this?
Ask students to add to their quick write by responding to the following: What do I want to know?
IDEAS FOR MODIFYING THIS STRATEGY
Model your own response to the lead.
Have students work in pairs.
Invite students to identify the kind of lead: dramatic, starting in the middle of a scene, leisurely, beginning at the end, introducing the narrator, misleading lead, ambiguous lead. (See Fletcher 1993 for descriptions of these types of leads.)
ASSESSMENT AND FEEDBACK
Ask students to share their initial response to the lead and their subsequent response.
Post students' "What do I want to know?" responses and refer to these as the reading of text continues.

After discussing the lead, we often continue reading the opening chapter aloud, pausing to ask questions and to highlight the writer's craft by noting word choice and lines that strike us. See more on this attention to craft in the "Reading with an Eye on Writing Craft" section, which starts on page 41. And we have found it effective to use these read-alouds to talk about our own process as readers. We think aloud (Tovani 2000, 26) using our "Kinds of Responses" to support our modeling. A number of texts have leads and first chapters that work well for read-alouds/think-alouds. In Figure 3.5 we have listed some of our favorite novels, shorts stories, and nonfiction memoirs and essays along with the "Kinds of Responses" think-alouds we model:

Figure 3.5

TITLE	AUTHOR	KINDS OF RESPONSES
Their Eyes Were Watching God (novel)	Zora Neale Hurston	Comprehension, Interpretive, Form/Craft
The House on Mango Street (novel)	Sandra Cisneros	Personal, Form/Craft
Fahrenheit 451 (novel)	Ray Bradbury	Comprehension, Form/Craft, Critical
"The Scarlet Ibis" (short story)	James Hurst	Interpretive, Form/Craft
"Letter from the Fringe" (short story)	Joan Bauer	Personal, Text to Text, Critical
"Harrison Bergeron" (short story)	Kurt Vonnegut	Comprehension, Interpretive, Form/Craft
"The Way Up to Heaven" (short story)	Roald Dahl	Interpretive, Form/Craft
"The Lottery" (short story)	Shirley Jackson	Comprehension, Form/Craft, Habits of Mind
"Bawlbaby" in *King of the Mild Frontier* (memoir excerpt)	Chris Crutcher	Form/Craft, Inspirational
"Being Mean" in *Living Up the Street* (memoir excerpt)	Gary Soto	Personal, Text to Text
Chapter 1 in *Black Boy* (memoir excerpt)	Richard Wright	Comprehension, Form/Craft, Critical
I Know Why the Caged Bird Sings (memoir)	Maya Angelou	Comprehension, Interpretive, Text to Text, Critical
"Corn-Pone Opinions" (essay)	Mark Twain	Form/Craft, Critical, Inspirational
"Hunter of Metaphors" (essay)	Ray Bradbury	Form/Craft, Inspirational, Habits of Mind
"Life of Prose and Poetry: An Inspiring Combination" (essay)	Marge Piercy	Form/Craft, Inspirational
"Mother Tongue" (essay)	Amy Tan	Comprehension, Form/Craft, Inspirational

But reading aloud is not limited to the lead. We have been surprised by the effectiveness of reading aloud throughout our exploration of a book. Typically we do the reading, pausing at key points to model our own thinking process as readers or asking students to share their thoughts.

Auditory and Visual Media in Support of Reading
We have also had great success with books on CD, read by authors or professional actors. The availability of these CDs at public libraries is helpful. We also appreciate the ready availability of podcasts (see http://www.openculture.com/freeaudiobooks). These tools allow us to be a fellow listener with our students. We embrace the use of MP3 players in support of listening as we read. There is a helpful list of literature podcasts available through iTunes at http://itunes.apple.com/us/genre/podcasts-arts-literature/id1401.

We want to tout the benefit of film in supporting close reading. The goal is not to have film take the place of reading, but to reinforce it. This focus on technology and film is consistent with IRA/NCTE standard 8: "Students use a variety of technological and informational resources (e.g., libraries, databases, computer networks, video) to gather and synthesize information and to create and communicate knowledge" (IRA/NCTE 1996, 3). See Chapter 7 for a discussion of using technology to "create and communicate knowledge."

We recognize that many of you are already using Shakespeare films in your classrooms. We share your appreciation for the role of film in support of reading literature. We have found it useful to show film clips before students read the scene or after they read the scene, and we have shown the film in its entirety before or after reading the play. We have listed below some of our favorite films of Shakespeare's plays, including modern adaptations.

> *Great Performances: Macbeth,* **2011, starring Patrick Stewart, and a modern adaptation,** *Scotland, PA,* **2002 (but we note this latter film is rated R because of language)**
> *A Midsummer Night's Dream,* **2003, with Kevin Kline, Calista Flockhart, and other delightful cast members, and a modern comedy about staging a musical version of the play at a high school,** *Get Over It,* **2001.**
> *Much Ado About Nothing,* **1998, directed by and starring Kenneth Branagh**
> *Othello,* **1995, starring Laurence Fishburne, Irene Jacob, and Kenneth Branagh, and a modern adaptation set in a high school,** *O,* **2001, which is rated R**
> *Richard III,* **1995, starring Ian McKellen and Annette Benning, and a documentary**

with Al Pacino about performing the play, *Looking for Richard*, 1996

Romeo and Juliet, **the Franco Zeffirelli version (1968), and Baz Luhrmann's film (1996)**

The Taming of the Shrew, **with Elizabeth Taylor and Richard Burton (1999). There is also a Broadway version on DVD, 2002. We also recommend the modern adaptation** *Ten Things I Hate About You*, **1999. In addition, there is a TV option, an episode of** *Moonlighting* **from season 3, "Atomic Shakespeare," which tells the story of** *The Taming of the Shrew*.

The Canadian TV series *Slings and Arrows* **is also a great option. It tells the humorous stories of a Shakespeare theater company and the challenges of mounting productions of various Shakespeare plays. Season 2 deals with a production of** *Macbeth*.

But we have also discovered film or TV that supports "reading" of other literature. The film version of *To Kill a Mockingbird* is a favorite choice. We also have seen the film *O Brother, Where Art Thou?* used to support students' reading and appreciation of *The Odyssey*. And we recommend the 2005 film version of *Pride and Prejudice*, starring Keira Knightley.

Surprising, at least for the two of us, are the literature possibilities in the animated TV show *The Simpsons*. As discussed earlier in this chapter, showing a *Simpsons* episode before students read a text can activate prior knowledge. The "Das Bus" episode (season 9) focuses on issues of survival that support students' thinking prior to reading *Lord of the Flies*. We have also used *The Simpsons* episode "Treehouse of Horror" (season 9) in conjunction with *The Crucible*. Poe's poem "The Raven" is highlighted in "Treehouse of Horror" (season 2) as well. "Tales from the Public Domain" (season 13) includes parodies of both *Hamlet* and *The Odyssey*. And in "Four Great Women and a Manicure" (season 20), Homer gets a part in *Macbeth* and then Marge takes on the persona of Lady Macbeth by encouraging Homer to assert his power with his fellow cast members. We appreciate and recommend high school teacher Ginger Eikmeier's article on using *The Simpsons* to support students' understanding of literature. As she notes, "Literary themes and references are prominent in pop culture, and without the knowledge of the original pieces of literature, we cannot fully participate in this culture" (2008, 79). And the laughter that happens while using *The Simpsons* in support of literature exploration is an added bonus!

Star Trek: The Next Generation also has a literature tie with the episode "Darmok," which includes a brief recounting of the epic "Gilgamesh." Clips of this scene can be found on YouTube.

In Chapter 7, we explore the use of film and video games created by students to show their understanding of literature.

CLOSE READING

In her book *Reading Like a Writer* Francine Prose speaks to the importance of close reading: "I read closely, word by word, sentence by sentence, pondering each deceptively minor decision the writer had made" (2006, 3).

We embrace close reading as a way to focus students' attention on the craft of writing.

Reading with an Eye on Writing Craft

A key to close reading is pace. We need to slow students down as they read and provide a focus that helps them see and appreciate each choice a writer makes. We embrace Tom Newkirk's definition of slow reading as "the relationship we have with what we read, with the quality of attention that we bring to our reading, with the investment we are willing to make." Newkirk calls on us as readers to "commit ourselves to follow a train of thought, to mentally construct characters, to follow the unfolding of an idea, to hear a text, to attend to language, to question, to visualize scenes" (2012, 2). To instill this habit of slowing down as readers requires practice and focused attention on the writer's craft.

Words

We often start our slow reading with a focus on words. As Prose puts it, "All the elements of good writing depend on the writer's skill in choosing one word instead of another" (2006, 16). To help with this effort, we ask students to focus on specific words or parts of speech in a chapter or excerpt.

Tom Romano writes about the importance of well-chosen verbs: "Verbs move forward writing. Verbs carry action. Verbs eliminate wasted energy and verbiage. Active verbs, my linguist friend Max Moorenberg says, move readers across the white space" (2004, 158). James Thurber's humorous story "The Catbird Seat" illustrates how well-chosen verbs can show us (or in this case, help us hear) character. In describing the speech of the character Mrs. Burrows, he uses *bounced brawled, romped,* and *catapulted* (Thurber 1952).

Tillie Olsen's story "I Stand Here Ironing" illustrates the impact of present-tense verbs: "Let her be. So all that is in her will not bloom—but in how many does it? There is still enough left to live by" (1995, 24).

In *The Great Gatsby*, F. Scott Fitzgerald uses verbs to help paint a picture of Nick's first encounter with Daisy: "gleaming, rippling, ballooned" (Prose 2006, 28).

We have found it helpful to have students make a list of the words they notice as they read. We have also had success with assigning students to read for parts of speech and then having them meet in small groups with other students who read for a different part of speech. Using sticky-note flags or highlighting the words in the text is helpful for this kind of close reading (see "Tracking as They Read" on page 53 for more on using these tools).

This emphasis on words also supports vocabulary development. Janet Allen reminds us that vocabulary instruction that "makes words meaningful, memorable, and useful begins with rich shared experiences," and that such experiences usually come from "texts that are chosen for common reading" (2007, 95–96).

Our goal is to get students to think about words, to respect the word choices made by the writers they read, to be attentive to their own word choices as writers, and perhaps even to fall in love with words. (We recommend Janet Allen's *Words, Words, Words* (2000) for ideas on helping students learn and perhaps love vocabulary.)

Sentences

"The well-made sentence transcends time and genre. A beautiful sentence is a beautiful sentence, regardless of when it was written, or whether it appears in a play or magazine article" (Prose 2006, 36). We invite students to build on their close reading of words by finding examples of "well-made sentences" in a text they are reading. We have students share these lines aloud so that we fill the classroom with "beautiful sentences."

We share Neil Postman's recognition of the importance of a well-written sentence: "There is no escaping the fact that when we form a sentence, we are creating a world. We are organizing it, making it pliable, understandable, useful" (1995, 84). We want students to look closely at how sentences are constructed—to determine what makes a good sentence (see Figure 3.6).

We also want to focus students' attention on sentences that address specific topics or themes. In *Speak* by Laurie Halse Anderson and *The Absolutely True Diary of a Part-Time Indian* by Sherman Alexie, the authors explore high school. Laurie Halse Anderson uses "Lies They Tell You in High School." For example, "We are here to help you." "You will have enough time to get to your class before the bell rings." "Your schedule was created with your needs in mind" (1999, 5–6).

Sherman Alexie's text talks about high school and a different set of rules: "The Unofficial and Unwritten (but you better follow them or you're going to get beaten twice as hard) Spokane Indian Rules of Fisticuffs." For example: "If somebody insults you, then you have to fight him." "If somebody insults any of your family or friends, or if you think they're thinking about insulting your family or friends, then you have to fight him." "You should never fight a girl, unless she insults you, your family or your friends, then you have to fight her" (2007, 61–62).

Figure 3.6

STRATEGY: SENTENCE STUDY
Write a sentence on the board from the text students are currently reading.
Ask students to list things they notice about the sentence.
Have students share their observations.
Ask students to find their own example of a well-written sentence from the text and share it in a small group.
Have each group select the "best sentence" from the group and present it to the class with their analysis of the sentence.
IDEAS FOR MODIFYING THIS STRATEGY
Provide students with the sentences to analyze.
Ask students to find sentences that illustrate specific examples of writing craft (see discussion that follows).
Make sentence study a regular routine and have students sign up to present a sentence to the class.
ASSESSMENT AND FEEDBACK
Collect students' sentence examples and note patterns in the sentences they have chosen. If necessary, follow up with individual students who may need additional support.
Evaluate group presentations of sentence study.
Assign participation points to students who present a sentence study.

Figurative Language

We want our students to see, hear, smell, and feel what they are reading. Figurative language taps into their sensory response. We invite students to read for examples of simile, metaphor, and personification. We also appreciate how figurative language shows the craft of writing. We want students to be able to identify examples of figurative language and discuss how these examples of craft support the elements of good stories. We focus here on figurative language in support of character and setting.

In Flannery O'Connor's (1971) short story "The Life You Save May Be Your Own," students explored the way we come to know the character of Mr. Shiftlet through simile: "The ugly words settled in Mr. Shiftlet's head like a group of buzzards in the top of a tree" (55). And this later simile, after Mr. Shiftlet has manipulated the old woman into paying for paint: "In the darkness Mr. Shiftlet's smile stretched like a weary snake waking up a fire" (64).

Kurt Vonnegut's (1998) short story "Harrison Bergeron" uses simile and metaphor to describe characters. For example: "A buzzer sounded in George's head" (47); "His thoughts fled in panic, like bandits from a burglar alarm" (48); "Her voice was a warm, luminous, timeless melody" (50).

In *Speak*, Anderson uses simile to show us how the narrator feels: "I have been dropped like a hot Pop Tart on a cold kitchen floor" (1999, 21).

John Updike's story "Man and Daughter in the Cold" illustrates the use of figurative language in describing the setting in a paragraph lead that paints a picture of the daughter skiing: "in air like slices of transparent metal interposed everywhere" (2004, 421).

Fitzgerald (1998) helps us experience the setting of his short story "Winter Dreams" with a simile, "The long Minnesota winter shut down like the white lid of a box," and personification, "The moon held a finger to her lips and the lake became a clear pool, pale and quiet."

Paragraphs and Structure

> *In general, remember that paragraphing calls for a good eye as well as a logical mind. Enormous blocks of print look formidable to readers, who are often reluctant to tackle them. Therefore, breaking long paragraphs in two, even if it is not necessary to do so for sense, meaning, or logical development, is often a visual help. But remember, too, that firing off many short paragraphs in quick succession can be distracting. . . . Moderation and a sense of order should be the main consideration in paragraphing*
>
> —Strunk and White (2007)

Structure matters. We want students to know this before they take on the task of structuring their own essays. We want them to notice long paragraphs and the single-sentence paragraph and consider how these choices impact them as readers.

Jane Austen draws us into her novel *Pride and Prejudice* with a one-sentence paragraph: "It is a truth universally acknowledged, that a single man in possession of a good fortune, must be in want of a wife" (2003, 5). The short story "Letter from the Fringe" by Joan Bauer also begins with a single sentence: "Today they got Sally" (2001, 181).

In contrast, Austen's (2004) lead in *Sense and Sensibility* is a lengthy paragraph in which she introduces the family of the Dashwoods and their estate. The novel *Atonement* (McEwan 2001) also begins with a lengthy paragraph, which describes the play the thirteen-year-old character, Briony, has written and is preparing to stage. It's our first glimpse into this character and illustrates her imagination as well as her need to get all of the details right.

We provide students with the opportunity to look closely at paragraphs as they read. We have also had success with a hands-on activity that provides students with multiple paragraphs and asks them to put them in an order that makes sense to them as readers (see Figure 3.7).

Figure 3.7

STRATEGY: CUTTING AND PASTING PARAGRAPHS
Provide students with envelopes containing a multi-paragraph excerpt from the text that has been cut into separate paragraphs.
Ask students to read each paragraph and arrange them in the order that makes sense to them as readers.
Have students then paste their version of the excerpt onto colored paper.
Provide students with a copy of the excerpt as it was originally written and have them note or highlight places where their order differs from the original.
IDEAS FOR MODIFYING THIS STRATEGY Provide different students with different excerpts.
Have students work in groups to put the excerpt in order.
ASSESSMENT AND FEEDBACK Collect students' pasted paragraphs to check their understanding of the paragraph order.
Ask students to write an exit note based on their experience of putting the excerpt back together again.

Close reading focuses students' attention on the choices authors make in crafting a text. But we also want students to discover the power of these choices—of language. "Language is for discovery . . . Language is our canoe up the wilderness river, our bush plane, our space capsule, our magic. Instead of 'now you see it, now you don't,' using language works in reverse: 'now you don't see it, now you do'" (Romano 2007, 170).

Reading with an Eye on Literary Structure
We build on the close reading for writing craft by focusing students on literary structure: the elements of a good story, novel, essay, memoir, or poem.

Character
As noted in our earlier discussion of character, we may assign (or invite students to choose) a character to track through the story or novel. They become the class expert on this character, noting how the author uses detail to help us see the character. We

have found it useful to use shorter texts as an introduction to character exploration.

For example, in Eudora Welty's short story "A Worn Path," we come to know the character of Phoenix Jackson as she makes the long, arduous journey to town: "She was very old and small and she walked slowly in the dark pine shadows, moving a little from side to side in her steps, with the balanced heaviness and lightness of a pendulum in a grandfather clock" (1982, 142). We want students to identify all of the ways characters come to life.

Figure 3.8 provides more information for how to focus students' attention on character details. We also reference Welty's story in support of students writing a character sketch in Chapter 7.

Figure 3.8

STRATEGY: CHARACTER DETAILS
Hand out a copy of a short story or an excerpt.
Ask students to note examples of details that help us see/know a character: appearance, including clothing; physical mannerisms, including facial expressions; and speech.
IDEAS FOR MODIFYING THIS STRATEGY
Have students work in groups; assign each group one of the character details columns: appearance, physical mannerisms, speech.
Have students use different-colored highlighters to mark character details. (See the section titled "Tracking as They Read" for more on using highlighters.)
Ask students to note use of similes in support of character detail.
ASSESSMENT AND FEEDBACK
Ask students to share examples from their character details columns.
Collect students' character details columns to check for what they recorded and anything they missed.

Setting

We briefly discussed setting in the section on figurative language (see page 41). But we want to revisit this important literary element because we have found that students' understanding of the reading is supported by being able to visualize where the story takes place.

As noted in the section titled "Tapping into Students' Background Knowledge" (see page 31), we have used photographs from the time period in which a story is set to create a visual image. For example, middle school teacher Lisa Souther sets up a photo gallery to allow students to see Harlem, where the stories in Walter Dean Myers's *145th Street* take place.

Plot

We have both been guilty of not giving enough attention to plot or of relying on comprehension quizzes to check for students' understanding of plot. But there are other strategies for exploring the sequence of events, specifically: slide show, haiku summary, plot bookmarks, and comic strip plots. These strategies are described in the following paragraphs, and details for slide show and haiku summary are given in Figures 3.9 and 3.10.

We are grateful, again, to Marisa Real for her reading strategies in support of plot: slide show and haiku summary.

Slide show provides students with the opportunity to work collaboratively to synthesize a section or chapter of a reading and then make their synthesis visual by having students depict a frozen scene (slide) of a key event with a narrator providing a voiceover to explain the "slide." (See Appendix B6, "Slide-Show Student Instructions" and Appendix B7, "Slide-Show Graphic Organizer.")

In the haiku summary activity, students use this poetic format to summarize a chapter or section of their reading. Marisa Real's students used this strategy while reading *To Kill a Mockingbird*. After students wrote and shared their haikus, they went to the hallway and posted their haikus, each of which represented a section of the book, in chronological order. Marisa provided us with the following student examples:

Folks holdin' grudges
Give others fright of hatred
Nothing good will come

Mortified tonight
A walking ham isn't fun
When you're being one

A night meant for fun
Will take a deadly turn
A hero revealed

Each student read aloud his or her haiku summary, and then Marisa read aloud the CliffsNotes summaries. Students preferred their haikus, which allowed them to discover or rediscover this poetic technique, but in the process of creating them they also reviewed plot details. (See Figure 3.10 for the haiku summary strategy details and Appendix B8 for a student instruction handout.)

Figure 3.9

STRATEGY: SLIDE SHOW

Form small groups of four or five students and assign each group different chapters or sections from the text they are reading.

Explain to students that they are going to create visual representations (slides) of key events in their chapter or section. Their goal is to illustrate plot.

Ask students to identify and write down the five to seven most important events or key moments in their assigned chapter or section.

Have students choose a narrator from their group who will do the voice-over for each slide during the presentation.

Students then make a list of all the characters involved in each of the key moments and decide on other details: costumes, setting details, and props.

Have students draw a quick sketch of each "key moment" slide (including where each character will stand).

Students then write the voice-over script for the slides. This should include a paraphrase of the text and should be at least three but no more than six sentences in length. Students should make sure the voice-over scripts are legible.

Students make any set pieces or props and arrange for costumes, including what needs to be brought from home.

Students practice the presentation of each of their slides with the voice-over.

Have students present their slide shows to the class.

IDEAS FOR MODIFYING THIS STRATEGY

Have students do fewer slides.

Have students draw their slides rather than act them out.

Have students rotate the role of narrator.

Assign each student a key scene and have each create a slide for that scene.

ASSESSMENT AND FEEDBACK

Assess slide-show presentations based on voice-over scripts and presentation.

Solicit individual student feedback regarding what students learned from their own slide show and/or what they learned from watching the slide-show presentations of their peers.

Figure 3.10

STRATEGY: HAIKU SUMMARY
Assign students chapters from a section of the novel they are reading.
Ask students to write two haikus to summarize the chapter they were assigned.
In class, have students write their haikus on separate slips of paper or sticky notes.
Have students then meet with a partner and put their haikus in chronological order. This pair then joins with another partner pair, and again they put their haikus in chronological order. This repeats until the whole class's haikus are in order.
The goal is to end up with all the haikus in chronological order and to read and discuss the haikus as a way to check comprehension and summarize the plot.

IDEAS FOR MODIFYING THIS STRATEGY
Have students work in small groups based on chapter assignments to write the haikus and/or put the haikus in chronological order.
After students have put all the haikus in the class in chronological order, post the haikus in a visible place to remind students of the plot.

ASSESSMENT AND FEEDBACK
Collect haikus to check comprehension. Follow up with students whose haikus suggest there may be concerns regarding comprehension.
Ask students to summarize in writing key plot points based on the haikus.
Have students write an exit note to check understanding and solicit feedback: What went well? What went less well?

Student teachers Kara McPhillips and Gabrielle Buvinger-Wild discovered the importance of supporting students' understanding of plot in *The Great Gatsby*. They developed and distributed a bookmark for students to use to note important events and supporting quotes. These bookmarks were printed on colored paper (see the reproducible template for these bookmarks in Appendix B9). Bookmarks like these can also be used to help students analyze theme (see the next section).

For what we refer to as the comic strip plot strategy, Kara and Gabrielle used a graphic organizer that asked students to identify key plot points in chronological order. They had students make a cartoon drawing for each key plot point to tap into students' visual learning (see template in Appendix B10). This strategy can be used for individual chapters or sections of a longer work. Students can work in groups, with each group member focusing on a different portion of the text. It also works well with short stories. (See Kara and Gabrielle's soundtrack assignment for *The Great Gatsby* in Chapter 7 for another strategy students can use to demonstrate their understanding of plot.)

Theme

Our hope is that students will understand that theme is more than the message or moral of the story. We want them to see theme as the "so what" of the story—to understand that theme is a lesson or lessons we learn from reading. We want students to dig into the text to look for the quotes that help to reveal the theme(s) as if they are uncovering the precious secret of the story. Reading for theme does not come easily; we have to work for it.

To help students begin to read for theme, we point out some quotes. Depending on what we know about students as readers and the complexity of the text, we may provide the quotes for students as they read. In this situation, we ask students to stop and pay close attention to the quote. Where is it located in the text? What does the quote tell us about the story? The characters? How does the quote connect with students' own lives? Is there a lesson in the quote? We have found this strategy helpful when students are reading longer texts.

But we also recognize the importance of students finding their own examples of quotes that highlight theme. So after some modeling of reading for theme, in which we point out quotes, we ask students to note quotes that they discover as they read—quotes that seem to be saying something important that goes beyond the story itself. For example, when reading Tillie Olsen's short story "I Stand Here Ironing," students pointed out this quote: "School was a worry to her. She was not glib or quick in a world where glibness and quickness were easily confused with ability to learn." Students can mark quotes with sticky notes, but we have also found that theme bookmarks (see Figure 3.11) work well.

Many of us are required to use literature anthologies. We know this can create challenges, as students are often resistant to textbooks, but we have found that the use of topics related to theme that organize short stories in an anthology can be used to support students' understanding of themes. For example, in a junior literature anthology, "modern" short stories were categorized by the following topics: "Passage and Change," "Psychological Insight," and "The Family." Knowing the topic in the anthology supported students in looking for theme.

We have used anthology organization by asking students to pick one of the anthology topics and focus their reading (or rereading) efforts on the themes in those stories, marking quotes that illustrated the theme. Teachers can also compile their own short-story groupings based on theme. For example, "Letter from the Fringe" by Joan Bauer, "Shortcut" by Nancy Werlin, and "The Pin" by Chris Crutcher are three stories that deal with identity and school.

Figure 3.11

STRATEGY: THEME BOOKMARK
Provide students with a bookmark on which to note quotes as they read for theme (see Appendix B9). As they read, have students write down quotes and/or page numbers of quotes that reveal theme. Have students share their quotes in small groups or in whole-class discussion.
IDEAS FOR MODIFYING THIS STRATEGY List some quotes related to theme on the bookmark before giving the bookmarks to students, and ask students to add more of their own quotes. Have students work in literature circles during the reading of the text and use the quotes and notes on the bookmarks to support literature circle discussions.
ASSESSMENT AND FEEDBACK Check students' bookmarks. Have students write an exit note in which they list one of the quotes they found and explain how it relates to theme.

We have seen both middle school and high school students respond well to the opportunity to show their thinking by creating a collage in support of theme (see Figure 3.12).

Figure 3.12

STRATEGY: COLLAGE THEME
Have students select a topic (from the anthology or based on class collections). Students should read or reread the story(ies) and identify quotes that represent the theme. Using the quotes, students find or draw pictures that illustrate the theme. Students then present their collage either to a small group or the whole class.
IDEAS FOR MODIFYING THIS STRATEGY Have students work in small groups and discuss the stories with regard to theme, and then develop a group collage.
ASSESSMENT AND FEEDBACK Have students write a reflection about the collage in which they explain their understanding of the theme, using quotes from the story(ies) and referencing the collage. Have students take notes on the collage presentations of their peers and then write a short reflection on their understanding of the themes based on the presentations.

Symbolism and Motifs

We want students to know and appreciate the use of symbols—people, places, or objects that represent something beyond themselves to illustrate abstract or complex ideas. We have focused students' attention on Janie's hair and/or the pear tree in *Their Eyes Were Watching God* by Zora Neale Hurston, Lennie's puppy and/or Candy's dog in *Of Mice and Men* by John Steinbeck, the tree in *Speak* by Laurie Halse Anderson, and the barn and/or the windmill in *Animal Farm* by George Orwell. But we take to heart Probst's reminder that we want students to

> **see that a symbol is not just a substitution of one thing for another but an association that invests an image with new meaning. . . . Rather than dutifully search for and define it, reducing it to a simple-minded equation, they are more likely to toy with it, explore it, and wonder about its ambiguities. (2005, 124)**

Using this exploratory approach to symbolism, we begin with poetry as our focus text. We marvel at the choices of poems we can use to teach symbolism and list just a few examples here. Frost's poem "Stopping By Woods on a Snowy Evening" provides the opportunity to look at "woods" as a symbol. And the symbol exploration could expand to "promises," "miles," and the "horse." We also appreciate the opportunity to explore the symbolism of "two roads" in Frost's poem "The Road Not Taken." Langston Hughes's poem "As I Grew Older" offers the symbol of the "wall," and his poem "Mother to Son" offers the "stairs." Kristi has used E. E. Cummings's poem "maggie and millie and molly and may" to introduce symbolism to freshmen. In the poem, each girl finds something on the beach that symbolizes her own personality. The flowers in Mary Oliver's poem "Poppies" serve as symbols for teachers who stand up as "tall poppies" to share their professional expertise. Kimberly posted the poem on her office wall as inspiration.

From symbolism, we often move to an exploration of motif, a recurring object, concept, or structure in literature. We have joined with students in examining the flute in *Death of a Salesman* by Arthur Miller, a number of motifs in *The Great Gatsby* by F. Scott Fitzgerald, including the green light, cars, and parties, the horizon in *Their Eyes Were Watching God* by Zora Neale Hurston, and names in *The House on Mango Street* by Sandra Cisneros.

In the section that follows, we discuss the use of tracking in exploring both symbolism and motif.

TRACKING AS THEY READ

Much has been written about the importance of annotating a text (Tovani 2000, 29–30; Burke 2000, 213–215). Experienced readers often write in or on a text, underlining key phrases and highlighting interesting ideas. We need to actively teach adolescent readers how to respond to a text while they read so that they mark key passages but do not end up highlighting or tabbing every page. We have had success with several approaches to marking the text. While some approaches work best with short texts and others with longer readings, especially homework reading assignments, all facilitate active, close reading and provide students with passages from the text to appreciate, examine, and return to when they are ready to write.

Underlining and Highlighting

The beauty of underlining and highlighting as basic responses to a text is that they can be either carefully guided or completely free-form, either helping students to see a pattern that we find important or crucial, or welcoming students to respond to any pattern they see. We have found success with beginning the year with guided highlighting/underlining and then gradually moving to a point where students can respond to any pattern they find. Guiding them through initial responses helps lay the groundwork for students to see and understand what is important in a text, then allows them to branch out. Students who are still developing reading and analytical skills can depend on the modeling we do, and students who are more confident in their skills can use our patterns as a springboard to find new details in a text.

Figures 3.13 and 3.14 describe two strategies for teaching students to use highlighting and underlining to analyze a text. Figure 3.13 describes using a short text, but we also appreciate the use of marking in support of reading longer texts, as described in Figure 3.14. Again, we have learned the importance of modeling this skill before we turn students loose with a stack of sticky notes and a novel.

As noted in the section titled "Reading with an Eye on Literary Structure," we want students to examine the use of symbols and motifs. Making this craft visible through highlighting and underlining supports this exploration.

Figure 3.13

STRATEGY: MARKING A SHORT POEM
Find a poem with rich imagery and give each student a copy.
Hand out several colors of colored pencils or highlighters.
After the poem has been read aloud several times (either by you, the teacher, by student volunteers, or with choral reading), ask students to use one color to underline or highlight images that appeal to their visual senses. Have students share responses, and have them use another color to underline images that appeal to a sense of touch, then smell, and so on. They should use a different color to highlight or underline images of different senses.
IDEAS FOR MODIFYING THIS STRATEGY
Model using the first color for the students, or do the first color together as a whole class, then have students work independently on the next color.
Have students work in pairs on the second color after modeling the first color.
Alter this lesson to teach about symbol, metaphor, simile, and so on.
ASSESSMENT AND FEEDBACK
Look over students' shoulders to determine what they are underlining or highlighting. Keep a running list, or have students make a list on the board, of ideas/topics they noted.
Have students hand in the underlining/highlighting and skim quickly to make sure they have the idea.
Discuss the poem. This activity should enable you to call on anyone in the room to share, as you will have checked to ensure they have all completed the underlining/highlighting.

We often follow the strategies described in Figures 3.13 and 3.14 with low-stakes writing. After marking the poem, students are asked to write about the imagery. After tracking the motifs, students write about how a motif adds to the setting, character, or theme. They might respond to the question, What predictions can you make based on the motif? (For more on low-stakes writing, see Chapter 4.)

Tabbing the Text Using Sticky Notes

Tabbing is a quick reference and visual reminder of what the author has accomplished; tabbing encourages rereading and reviewing and gathering quotations in service of a more formal analysis.

Again, we've learned the importance of actively teaching and modeling the usefulness of sticky notes in a text as tabs. Simply requiring students to insert a sticky every time they "like" a line will neither support their thinking nor help them understand the purpose of marking a text. And we feel compelled to share the cautionary tale of Rob Vaughn, a student teacher working with sixth graders. His students used sticky notes to mark themselves, the desks, and each other rather than the text. He wisely advises that specific directions regarding what to "tab" be stated before handing out any materials. We have found it useful to pause at multiple points throughout the reading of a text to review what has been marked, why, and how that information can be used. Note: Kristi asked her students to tab key passages in texts for a year before she tried doing it herself, only to find that she was so distracted by tabbing that she lost sight of the story. So she stopped tabbing after a few chapters (which her students will do, too, if she doesn't constantly check in and review its purpose).

Figure 3.14

STRATEGY: MARKING MOTIFS IN A NOVEL OR PLAY
Hand out a photocopy of the first few paragraphs or pages of a novel or play that is to be studied.
Provide students with a list of motifs that they will see in the text selection.
Ask students to underline the motifs where they appear in the photocopies.
Discuss students' findings: Does the motif seem to enhance character? Setting? Using the motif as a starting point, what predictions do students have about the text? What can they say about the author's style?
IDEAS FOR MODIFYING THIS STRATEGY
Model the underlining of one motif and share your predictions, then ask students to do the same for a second.
Assign different motifs to different students, then have students work and share in groups or with partners.
Alter this lesson to teach about details in setting, imagery, tone, character, and so on.
Modify the length of the text selection, depending on students' ability level. For example, we have had success with several pages for older students and one paragraph for younger students.
Have students track motifs for the rest of the text in preparation for a formal written response.
Use a short story or short essay and complete the reading and highlighting of motif in class.
ASSESSMENT AND FEEDBACK
Have students hand in their annotated text. Skim this work to see patterns and to determine whether follow-up is needed with the whole group or individuals.
Ask students to share with a partner or small group and report back to the class any connections they find in their underlining.

A strategy to address the "tabs are too distracting" dilemma is to focus students' efforts. Ask students to tab two details and then refer to the details they have tabbed when they participate in a discussion. In this way, students can see the usefulness of tabbing. Figure 3.15 describes other ideas for focusing students' tabbing. Sharing our own stories of limited tabbing helps students focus their efforts on tabbing one or two details rather than four or five in a story or chapter. Their focus is clearer and this ultimately supports their writing by helping students narrow their options. Most novels we teach are too "big"; students can't see everything, especially in one reading. Tabbing creates snapshots of the text as they read.

One of Kristi's students showed her carefully tabbed novel and shared how it helped her both focus and track her reading. She then went on to note, as she ran her fingers over the tabs, the tactile benefit of tabbing: "It's like a car wash for my hands."

REREADING

It is a truth universally acknowledged that we discover something new with each reading of a text. Kimberly sees new details about characters each time she reads *Pride and Prejudice*. She also rediscovers her admiration of Austen's wit. And Kristi enjoys the opportunity to see something new with each reading of *The Hours* by Michael Cunningham. How did a man writing about women get it so right?

We also reread texts each time we teach them, and with each rereading our understanding of the text deepens. Kristi has taught Toni Morrison's *Song of Solomon* nine times and has found something new to track and comment on every time. Kimberly has taught *Speak* to graduate students preparing to be secondary English teachers for the past nine years, and with each rereading she discovers something new about the narrator and Laurie Halse Anderson's writing craft. And both of us are informed by the opportunity to explore a book we have read with a new group of students.

We worry about how assigning texts to grade levels sends students the message that there is no value in rereading a text. What would happen if students read *To Kill a Mockingbird* in middle school and again in high school? A high school student who read the novel as an eighth grader and then again as a tenth grader noted, "Because I knew the story and already knew what was going to happen, I could focus on the smaller details: Boo Radley, the relationships between characters, and even the trial. I could also appreciate the way the story is written. It's kind of like watching a movie again, where you see all the things you missed the first time around." A student who had read *Speak* on her own as a sixth grader and then reread it with her class as a freshman was struck by how differently she felt about the text after the second reading. She had a new appreciation for the writing craft, in particular noting the ever-changing mascot and the irony of the "symbolism" in Melinda's English class and Melinda's own use of symbolism in telling her story. "And," the student pointed out, "I could also relate it to more because I was in high school and reading about high school."

Figure 3.15

TEACHING STRATEGY: TABBING WITH STICKY NOTES AND A FOCUS
After introducing specific images, symbols, motifs, or themes in a text (see "Reading with an Eye on Literary Structure"), have students do one of the following focused tabbing activities:
Group students according to the literature structure they are tabbing and have them meet daily to discuss what they have tabbed and why.
Ask students to track several (limit the number to two or three) images/symbols/motifs/ themes and use different-colored tabs for each one.
Assign one image, symbol, motif, or theme and ask students to track it *and* to tab passages that confuse or intrigue them so that they can discuss it in class. Have them use one color for the assigned image/symbol/motif/theme and one color for discussion ideas.
Push students to write a follow-up question on the sticky-note tab itself rather than in a journal. This works best if students are tabbing only one idea. (We have found large arrow sticky notes work well for this. Students use them to tab the section and to make notes.)

IDEAS FOR MODIFYING THIS STRATEGY
Limit the number of ideas to track.
Tab the first chapter and walk students through what you have done and why. Use this modeling as a starting point and then work as a whole class or in small groups to tab the next chapter or section. This can work well with shorter novels and with groups of struggling readers.

ASSESSMENT AND FEEDBACK
Check in with students frequently. We have learned that if we require tabbing rather than suggest tabbing, we must determine a way to assess it and check in with students regarding their progress.
Use tabs as a jumping-off point for discussion (see the section on discussion in Chapter 4).
Randomly collect a few students' tabbed novels at the beginning of class to assess tabbing. We keep a list of students to ensure we check tabbing for each one over the course of reading the novel.
Tie journal assignments directly to what students are tabbing. Require them to use the information they have tabbed as evidence to support their ideas in journal entries. (See Chapter 4 for more on journal writing.)

We want students to join us in the discoveries that rereading offers. Within our classrooms, we have found that asking students to return to sections or chapters of a text they have read to dig deeper is at first met with resistance, but with time and practice, students recognize the "ahas" that come with rereading. We concur with Sheridan Blau's endorsement of rereading: "I want to assert, in fact, that rereading is the most powerful strategy available to all readers for helping themselves read more profitably, especially when they are reading difficult texts" (2003, 143–143). In fact, Kristi has experimented with having her senior students read the year's assigned novels during the preceding summer. Students were not required to write in response— yet. The first reading helped them to get a sense of the trajectory of the story and to meet the characters. Most important, it helped them begin the class study of the novels with their own questions. They came ready to learn why a certain confusing scene was central to the story or to explore what frustrated them in the first reading. Also, knowing the end of the book helped them to see how the author used the first paragraphs and first chapter to introduce the reader to themes, motifs, and ideas that coalesce in the final scenes. Students who completed the initial reading and the rereadings of texts had a deeper appreciation for the work of writing a novel.

The decision about how to support reading and rereading depends on the text and what we know about our students as readers. We have read a text or an excerpt from a text aloud and then asked students to go back and reread, paying attention to details of structure and/or writing craft. And we have focused their attention on characters, setting details, what they know so far regarding the plot, or their initial impressions regarding theme. We have also structured multiple readings of a short text. This works particularly well with poetry (see Figure 3.16).

As we shared ideas and wrote this chapter about "reading like a writer," we were struck by the importance of this stance. Our hope is that students will discover all that literature has to offer: expansion of their knowledge of culture and history; opportunities to develop empathy for characters, situations, and the lives of others; and enlargement of their own vision of life's possibilities. We realize that we are living in a time when much of the focus of teaching is on skills, accountability, and preparing kids for the workplace. We have heard the criticisms of devoting time to reading and writing about literature. And we are prepared to join with our fellow English/language arts teachers in defense of the study of literature. Reading and writing about literature provides students with the opportunity to read for understanding and detail, to frame questions, to frame an argument and prove it with support from the text, to develop critical-thinking skills, and to expand their knowledge of grammar and conventions. But reading and writing about literature does more:

> **We need literature to learn to get along. Literature and life converge in the field of human relationships. What characterizes quality literature—refusal to stereotype or generalize, fidelity to the whole complicated truth in all its breadth and subtlety, energy and inventiveness, eloquence, paying careful attention, discomfort at pat answers, and a generosity and sympathy with others—also characterizes a thoughtful life. (Gillespie 1994, 21)**

We have had the privilege of witnessing students wrestle with the big questions of life in the literature that they read, make connections to their own lives, and discover the tenacity needed to craft writing that captures their thinking. It is challenging, complex, and worthy work.

Figure 3.16

STRATEGY: REREADING A POEM
Provide a copy of a poem for each student.
Ask students to read the poem and mark words or phrases they admire.
Ask students to reread the poem and note in a different color words or lines that they do not understand.
Read the poem aloud to students and ask them to pay particular attention to the places they have marked.
Place students in small groups and have them share the words or phrases they admire as well as discuss words and phrases that they do not understand.
Have groups then report their discoveries about the poem to the whole class.

IDEAS FOR MODIFYING THIS STRATEGY
Model the steps you want students to complete by reading a poem aloud and marking it so students can see what is expected.
Provide several different poems. After students have completed the first two readings, have them form groups with students who have the same poem, read it aloud within the group, and then hold the discussion.

ASSESSMENT AND FEEDBACK
Circulate and observe students as they mark the poem.
Collect students' "marked" poems.
Ask each group to summarize their discoveries in writing before they report to the whole group.
Require students to write an exit note in which they write examples of words/phrases they admired, words/phrases that confused them initially, and what they now understand about the confusing words/phrases.

CHAPTER 4

WRITING AND DISCUSSION IN SUPPORT OF THINKING

In Chapter 3, "Reading Like a Writer," we described ways to introduce students to key concepts in a text and provide a general framework and purpose for reading. When we dream big, it's our hope that students will then discover what Roger Rosenblatt writes about in his chapter titled "Writing Like a Reader":

> **You read something you admire as a writer, and you tend to take on the skin of the person who writes it. You see how the writer came up with what you're reading. You can sense another mind making this choice and that. In that way, every time you sit down to write, you're in the company of writers who have written before you. (2011, 111)**

With this dream in mind, in this chapter, as well as in Chapters 5, 6, and 7, we turn our attention to guiding students to "write like readers" by describing a variety of responses to texts. But we need a starting place. Whether they read an entire novel as homework, a short story or poem on their own in class, or a drama aloud during class time, students need us to model our thinking processes throughout a text and to guide their own processes. Asking students to write during reading provides a low-stakes forum for strengthening their abilities to analyze what they read, to identify and develop their own opinions about what is important in a text, and to discuss the text with genuine understanding and curiosity. Low-stakes writing during reading also provides teachers insight into students' comprehension and analysis and moves us away from rote reading quizzes and discussion questions.

In *Writing to Learn: Assigning and Responding to Writing Across the Disciplines* (1997), Peter Elbow argues that low-stakes writing provides a foundation for students' learning:

1.   *Frequent low-stakes assignments get students to keep up with the assigned reading every week.*

2.   *Low-stakes writing helps students be active learners. During low-stakes writing, virtually all minds are actively processing the ideas of the course.*

3.   *Low-stakes writing helps students find their own language for the issues of the course; they work out their own analogies and metaphors for academic concepts.*

4.   *Low-stakes writing improves the quality of students' high-stakes writing.*

5.   *With frequent low-stakes pieces, we ensure that students have already done lots of writing before we have to grade a high-stakes piece—so that they are already warmed up and fluent in their writing.*

6.   *Low-stakes writing gives us a better view of how students are understanding the course material and reacting to our teaching. We get a better sense of how their minds work.*

This chapter explores several options for low-stakes literature journal writing that reflect Elbow's goals. And with regard to Elbow's fourth goal, we posit that these writing strategies may become isolated assignments *or* crucial preparation for a high-stakes final paper. (See Chapters 5, 6, and 7 for a discussion of high-stakes writing assignments.) We keep in mind the definitions provided by Purves, Rogers, and Soter of "impressionistic" and "analytic" responses and the importance of requiring both in our classrooms:

> **If impressionistic, the focus will be less on the literary work than on the reader's subjective *reaction* to it. If analytic, the focus shifts from the reader's self to the literary work—that is, we write *about* the literary work rather than how we feel or think in reaction to it. . . .**
>
> **The analytic or text-examining response might be termed an intellectual one in which the reader attempts to distance himself or herself from the literary work. We might add, however, that not allowing adolescents the opportunity to articulate their impressionistic or self-examining responses to literary works can hamper subsequent analytic responses. (1995, 161)**

Thus, the strategies and examples that follow can help students develop their impressionistic responses. Such responses can be a valuable end on their own, but can also help students move forward to more considered analytic responses. Once students know what specific aspects of a text pique their individual curiosity, they are more prepared to analyze using their own intellect and voice.

LITERATURE JOURNALS

As discussed in Chapter 3, underlining, highlighting, and tabbing are essential tools to facilitate close reading and push students to notice a writer's style and form an opinion about that style. A journal, then, can be a perfect way for students to make meaning of details they have underlined, highlighted, and tabbed. It is a place to practice writing about the text, to record first impressions, and to slowly develop an analysis that will become a polished written response. As our colleagues and we can attest, however, it is easy to assign journals but truly a challenge to make them meaningful. We may struggle with how free-form or scripted a journal should be, and we definitely question whether or not we can respond to all of that writing. In this chapter we offer some suggestions for crafting journal assignments that both guide students' reading and provide a space for them to come to their own conclusions about a text. We also offer simple feedback suggestions that will help us value student insights while being realistic about our ability to respond to everything that students write.

Over the years we have tried a variety of organization strategies for literature journals. We now require students to keep a journal specifically for their literature class; spiral notebooks work best. We keep extra notebooks on hand for students who cannot afford to buy their own journals and for students who have lost journals. We have experimented with requiring students to leave journals in carefully marked crates and folders in class, and we have sometimes required students to take journals home to complete a homework assignment. How we choose to organize journals depends on our students and may vary from class to class over the course of a day. But we know that creating a system that works for us and our students is critical to a successful literature workshop. (For more ideas on managing journals, see Atwell 1998, Christenbury 2006, and Rief 1992.)

Caroline O'Neill, one of Kristi's colleagues at United Nations International School in New York, makes an important suggestion about assigning journals: determine whether you will provide *strict, minimal,* or *independent* requirements for a journal. You may start with strict requirements and move to few requirements over the course of a novel or over the course of a semester. Or you may move in the other direction when you realize your students need more structure from you. The key is to understand that students need your guidance, but that it is perfectly all right to move away from or toward a structured approach, depending on their responses. Journals have been crucial to supporting our unit plans as well, as we often tie journal assignments directly to unit objectives and assign journals that help guide students to notice aspects of the text that they will write about in a final paper or project. To streamline our discussion of journals in this chapter, we provide descriptions and examples of each of O'Neill's suggested structures, and then offer modifications and assessment and feedback ideas that can work with all journal assignments, regardless of structure. We note that, as in other chapters of this book, we have researched, honored, built on, and modified the work of fellow teachers as we strive to find what works best for our students. Throughout this chapter, we give credit to sources and note where we have modified their assignments.

Journals with Strict Requirements

Journals with strict requirements allow for direct instruction with complex texts but still give students room to explore their own responses. Every year we work with developing readers, those students who need our help structuring their reading. We help them visualize what they read, make connections among texts, and activate background knowledge as they read. Our experience has shown us that journals with strict requirements particularly help developing readers by giving them something to look for, a specific problem to solve. Often these guided journals enable students to discover for the first time that a text can have a deeper meaning beyond the plot. Because these journals teach students what it is possible to see in a text, they can become much-needed scaffolding that supports readers who are just learning to comprehend and ponder the complexities of a text.

We have had success using this approach with developing readers, and near the beginning of the year with more mature readers. We have seen structured journals benefit students in the following ways:

- Help students to see that literature is more fun, interesting, complex, and challenging when we learn how to uncover its many layers
- Enable students to feel successful as they learn to read complex texts
- Give students something specific to discuss
- Model a vocabulary for the discussion of literature
- Create high expectations for literary response. When students must respond to complex questions, they move beyond writing simple statements and toward explaining *why* they believe what they believe about a text.

We trust teachers' creativity in modifying and developing the structured journal assignment ideas provided in this chapter to support their unique students. In addition, we recommend *Writing About Literature* (Johannessen, Kahn, and Walter 2009), which contains research-based methods for crafting unit plans and several sample unit plans with journal assignments.

Structured journals can take the form of graphic organizers, and we have used these to give students specific questions to answer *as they read*, because we do not find that all of the important questions are posed in class the day after a chapter is read. We include the example in Figures 4.1a and 4.1b to show how a structured journal can guide students to analyze quotations, and to show how an already strong assignment can be modified to meet students' needs. We owe the original idea to Oakland teacher Erin Carlson. When Kristi used it with developing readers, she realized they needed even more direct instruction to respond to the complex writing in *The House on Mango Street* by Sandra Cisneros. The original journal is shown in Figure 4.1a, and Kristi's modifications are shown in Figure 4.1b.

Both formats of the journal provide a quotation for students and guide them through what they should notice. Students have some freedom to make their own connections and to determine the significance of the passage. The second journal breaks down the concept just a bit more, defining the questions in specific terms that will, ideally, push students past superficial responses. This assignment can be modified even further, by requiring students to respond to only one question in the second column, for example. Because Kristi's *The House on Mango Street* unit aimed to teach students how to discuss important quotations, the journal helped students practice articulating what makes a quotation significant. The final assignment, an analytical paper, built directly on the quotations and responses students had written in their journals during their reading.

Journals with strict requirements might also take the form of directed questions to be answered either with homework reading or during class time. Students' answers to these questions can become drafts for a final assignment, and we can use their responses to help us determine what else they need from us on the path to understanding a text. We have had success with such question-and-answer journals and with the types of strictly structured journals listed in Figure 4.2.

Figure 4.1a

TWO-COLUMN QUOTATION AND RESPONSE JOURNAL

QUOTATION	RESPONSE
from the vignette "A House of My Own" Not a flat. Not an apartment in back. Not a man's house. Not a daddy's. A house all my own. With my porch and my pillow, my pretty purple petunias. My books and my stories. My two shoes waiting beside the bed. Nobody to shake a stick at. Nobody's garbage to pick up after. Only a house quiet as snow, a space for myself to go, clean as paper before the poem. (Page 108)	Speaker: Situation: Significance: Stylistic devices: Connections:

Figure 4.1b

MODIFIED TWO-COLUMN QUOTATION AND RESPONSE JOURNAL

QUOTATION	RESPONSE
from the vignette "A House of My Own" Not a flat. Not an apartment in back. Not a man's house. Not a daddy's. A house all my own. With my porch and my pillow, my pretty purple petunias. My books and my stories. My two shoes waiting beside the bed. Nobody to shake a stick at. Nobody's garbage to pick up after. Only a house quiet as snow, a space for myself to go, clean as paper before the poem. (Page 108)	Speaker: *WHO* is speaking? Situation: *WHEN* does this passage occur? *WHO* is involved? *WHAT* is happening? Significance: *WHAT* does the quotation mean? Try to include your own predictions. *HOW* does it connect to the rest of the novel? Consider characters, theme, and conflict. *WHY* is this quotation important? Is it a turning point? Stylistic devices: Do you see metaphors, alliteration, personification, sensory details? Connections: *HOW* does this quotation connect to themes we have discussed? To other quotations?

Figure 4.2
IDEAS FOR STRICTLY STRUCTURED JOURNAL ASSIGNMENTS

Guiding students to an important passage and asking for a specific response (similar to the example in Figure 4.1b):

Read and reread Hamlet's soliloquy at the end of act 2, scene 2. Paraphrase the lines, and then discuss how Shakespeare incorporates the idea of acting/performance to reveal Hamlet's self-doubt.

Quote the paragraph that first introduces Curley's wife to readers of *Of Mice and Men*. How does Steinbeck use color to characterize her?

Connecting assigned tabbing/highlighting (see Chapter 3) to journal writing:

Track an assigned character throughout a text or a specific chapter. List assigned quotations regarding that character and comment on his/her development. Do the same with motif, symbol, etc.

Preparing students for an impressionistic response:

Keep a diary using an assigned character and his/her reactions to assigned events. (*For example, in a unit on* Adventures of Huckleberry Finn, *teachers might ask students to record Jim's internal dialogue in response to (1) his first encounter with Huck, (2) the discovery of Huck's father, and (3) losing their way in the fog.*)

The possibilities are endless. It should be noted that we usually model these assignments for students. We start the unit by doing one journal assignment for them, then we do one as a class, then we set them free to do their own. (In Appendix C1, we provide an example of journal guidelines for a key passage analysis.) We collect student models of the independent journals and share them along the way, constantly reminding students of what appropriate, complex, and engaging responses look like. We have found that if we assign and model structured journals when students are still learning the basics in literary response, we can eventually begin to pull away some of the scaffolding, allowing them to choose their own quotations and then their own free-form response. We can move to assigning journals with minimal requirements, then to assigning independent journals.

Journals with Minimal Requirements

For teachers who shy away from direct instruction, strictly structured journals may seem too prescriptive. But we try to remember, our students are *our* students; we will know best if they need specific guidelines from us or if they are ready to branch out on their own and find meaning without our voices in their ears. If students are ready to start responding with more independence, assigning journals with minimal requirements will allow them more freedom yet still capitalize on our (their teachers') experience as readers and analyzers of text to guide them to important details and structure key questions. In the following sections we include examples of minimally structured journals that have been very successful in our classrooms.

The Three-Part Journal

This journal capitalizes on Kimberly's "rule of three," which comes from the concept of "triangulation" in qualitative research. Three different options stimulate students' complex thinking without overwhelming them with possibilities. The following journal framework has worked well in our classrooms:

> *Part 1:* **Three bullet points of summary (This provides a forum for summarizing but ensures that the journal is not all summary.)**
> *Part 2:* **Three "golden lines" (These can be lines students love, lines that they want to discuss, or lines that seem important to the story in some way.)**
> *Part 3:* **One evaluative question (see "Developing Questions" in Chapter 5) and one answer**

Ways to frame a three-part journal are as endless as each teacher's imagination. We typically keep parts 1 and 2 as they are described in the preceding list, although we may expand beyond the "rule of three." We like to give students an opportunity to summarize and record what they remember and to pull lines that strike their unique imaginations. Part 3 has proven the most flexible component. We have experimented with the following options for part 3: develop an analysis of one of the "golden lines"; analyze one character's (assigned or unassigned character) actions in this chapter; discuss the development of a motif (assigned or unassigned motif) in this chapter; write a one-paragraph personal response to an event (assigned or unassigned event) in this chapter. We find that a journal assignment in several parts provides structure but also allows for creativity and independent thought (See "Three-Part Journal Sample Requirements and Sample Entry" in Appendix C2.)

The Bookmark-Guided Journal

This idea builds on the use of bookmarks that we discussed in Chapter 3. The bookmark-guided journal allows us to guide students' reading, but still gives students some freedom in determining what is most important for response. We give students a bookmark with questions/directives to respond to over the course of the book. The bookmark format keeps the questions close at hand while students read and reminds them of what to look for in the text. We have used the following variations in structuring this journal:

- Provide a list of questions that must be answered at some point during the reading of a book, with each question answered only once. Students choose which question to connect to a particular day of reading. For example, one question might be, "How does a descriptive passage in this chapter emphasize the importance of setting to the story?" One student may write in response to this question for chapter 1, another student for chapter 8. Students can compare notes and make connections across the novel.
- Provide a list of characters on the bookmark. Ask students to respond to a different character in each chapter.
- Ask students to write a key quotation (usually one or two lines from the first chapter) on a bookmark. Ask them to draw connections to that quotation in each reading. Alternatively, teachers may assign a quotation. This assignment works best with shorter texts.
- Ask students to choose a quotation and analyze a specific aspect of it (style, for example) in their notebooks. On the bookmark, provide a model for such an analysis, so they always have the expectations close at hand.

As with the three-part journal, the only limits to bookmark-guided journals are a teacher's imagination and expectations. (See the sample bookmark in Appendix C3.)

Often, we determine that once students are able to meet the objectives of a unit with a minimally guided journal, they are ready to move to independent response. This, as always, varies from class to class and unit to unit.

Independent Journals

Independent journals can be liberating for students and teachers and can allow students to explore their own reactions to a text. Still, we have found it imperative to have our unit plans and final products, if any, in mind to ensure that we are still guiding students toward a reaction and/or interpretation that suits a unit's objectives. The following list provides ideas for independent journals that have worked in our classrooms. It is important to note that we have had the most success allowing developing readers to respond independently to shorter texts, as they learn that their independent responses are valued but do not feel overwhelmed with free-form assignments for complex texts. And we often push more mature readers to craft independent journals in response to longer texts, encouraging them to take more risks with challenging material.

INDEPENDENT JOURNALS THAT HAVE WORKED WELL WITH DEVELOPING READERS
- Students copy passages from a short story or poem, for example Edgar Allan Poe's "The Fall of the House of Usher," that they consider beautiful, disturbing,

inspiring, or even confusing. Students explain their reaction. Another option is to provide the passages and ask students to respond.

- In each chapter of a short novel, students write about their reactions to a character of their choice. For example, students might choose to respond to the possible innocence or guilt of a character of their choice in each chapter of Walter Dean Myers's *Monster*.

INDEPENDENT JOURNALS THAT HAVE WORKED WELL WITH MATURE READERS

- The "list" journal: This journal was born of Kristi's observations of what kind of notes she kept while she read a novel. She shared these notes with students and they asked if they could structure their journals in the same way. The requirements are slim: Keep a running list of page numbers of important quotations, lists of questions about quotes, and lists of general questions. Share them in discussion and add notes during class time. This method works well for initial readings of texts and should be modeled and shared. (See the "List Journal Sample" in Appendix C4 to note the ways that one student was able to use this type of journal to track events and to then develop an independent journal response based on the list.)
- Key issue journal: In this journal, students help determine, after the first chapter of a text, the key issues in a text. These often take the form of simple observations or questions, such as "The narrator confuses me," or "The women are all so weak." With help from the teacher, students reframe these issues into a focal point: What is the narrator's role? Or, How does gender affect characters' actions? Students then respond to one of these issues.

Journal Methods Summarized

Sometimes the mere fact that students are reacting to a text feels like enough for us. We have learned to channel this excitement into helping students structure assignments and transform their gut reactions into more considered responses. We recognize that the methods we've outlined—journals with strict requirements, journals with minimal requirements, and independent journals—can overlap, and do overlap in our classrooms. Teaching literature is, of course, a messy business, especially when we wish to provide room for independent response. As such, we provide a summary of methods in Figure 4.3, to be used as a quick reference to aid planning.

Figure 4.3
LITERATURE JOURNAL METHODS FOR QUICK REFERENCE

GUIDING STUDENTS TO A CLOSE ANALYSIS OF THE TEXT		
STRICT REQUIREMENTS (respond to *this* passage *in this way*) Read and reread Hamlet's soliloquy at the end of act 2, scene 2. Paraphrase the lines, and then discuss how Shakespeare uses specific images to reveal Hamlet's self-doubt. Quote the paragraph that first introduces Curley's wife to readers of *Of Mice and Men*. How does Steinbeck use color to characterize her?	**MINIMAL REQUIREMENTS** (respond to *this* passage) Read and reread Hamlet's soliloquy at the end of act 2, scene 2. Paraphrase the lines, and then discuss how Shakespeare uses imagery to reveal Hamlet's state of mind. Quote the paragraph that first introduces Curley's wife to readers in *Of Mice and Men*. How does Steinbeck characterize her?	**INDEPENDENT JOURNAL** (respond to *a* passage) Quote a passage from act 2 that reveals Hamlet's state of mind. Discuss what is revealed and how. Look carefully at how Steinbeck introduces his characters. Quote one example, and discuss what we learn about the character based on how he/she enters the scene.
CONNECTING ASSIGNED TABBING/HIGHLIGHTING (SEE CHAPTER 3) TO JOURNAL WRITING		
STRICT REQUIREMENTS Track your assigned character throughout a text or a specific chapter. Record assigned quotations regarding that character and comment on his/her development. (*Alternatively, do the same assignment with motif, symbol, etc.*)	**MINIMAL REQUIREMENTS** Track a character of your choice throughout a text or a specific chapter. Find and list relevant quotations regarding that character, and comment on his/her development. (*Alternatively, do the same assignment with motif, symbol, etc.*)	**INDEPENDENT JOURNAL** Use a list journal to determine the importance of a character in the text. What are you responding to most often? Why? (*Alternatively, do the same assignment with motif, symbol, etc.*)
PREPARING STUDENTS FOR AN IMPRESSIONISTIC RESPONSE		
STRICT REQUIREMENTS Keep a diary, writing in the voice of an assigned character and his/her reactions to assigned events. (*For example, in a unit on* Adventures of Huckleberry Finn, *teachers might ask students to record Jim's internal dialogue in response to (1) his first encounter with Huck, (2) the discovery of Huck's father, and (3) being lost in the fog.*)	**MINIMAL REQUIREMENTS** Keep a diary using a character's reaction to different events. (*For example, in a unit on* Adventures of Huckleberry Finn, *teachers might ask students to record Jim's internal dialogue in response to significant events.*)	**INDEPENDENT JOURNAL** Choose an important character in the text and keep a diary from his/her perspective.

Assessing Literature Journals

Over the course of a literature unit, journals can be assigned as homework or can be written in class, or assignments can be structured to include a combination of both. Although challenging, it is important that students keep all of their work in one notebook so that these during-reading writings can support students' thinking on final papers. Requiring continuous response to a text does pose a problem: how to grade all of that writing?

We have evidence that students will write and keep writing, even if we do not read every single page. But their thoughts do deserve feedback, validation, and correction. We have found the following methods of assessment useful when assigning journals:

- Stamp, every day, at the bottom of the entry so we know how much was completed. We note each journal assignment in the grade book immediately rather than collecting them at the end of the unit, which enables us to track completion and communicate with students and parents about the writing done during the unit *before* the final paper is assigned.
- Collect journals for one-third of the class one day, one-third the next, and so on. We ask students to highlight or underline their favorite lines for our response. Or, we have them write one question that remains in their mind, and we respond to this question.
- Ask students to respond verbally or in writing to one another's journals. Sometimes we assign one specific partner for an entire unit of study, and sometimes we pair them randomly on different days.
- Ask students to structure their journals in three columns: one column for a quoted passage, one for their response, and one for a partner's or our response. This allows students to receive feedback from us *or* from a peer.

Of course, as students track important concepts, they will need to discuss these concepts with other students. We often use journals as a springboard for discussion. The following section directly addresses methods for incorporating journals into class time. Requiring the use of journals for discussion helps us to check that the work is completed without collecting every journal every day, and ensures that all students have something to say.

CLASSROOM DISCUSSION

Discussion about literature is crucial in our classrooms. It helps facilitate understanding, develops independence, and allows students to learn from their peers. In fact, research shows that when students can discuss the texts they read, they develop their own insights more solidly and clearly than if they are simply *spoken to* in a language arts classroom (Blau 2003; Booth 1988; Burke 2003; Christenbury 2006; Christenbury and Kelly 1993; Probst 2007). Yet as language arts teachers, we face many barriers to holding effective classroom discussions: scheduling and administrative concerns, such as large class sizes and short class periods; unpredictable group chemistry, such as students who dominate and students who retreat during discussion; and our own teacher preparedness issues, such as grading techniques and struggling to "think on our feet" amidst discussion. Add to these the problem of students who did not do the reading and we can see why so many of us struggle with effective discussion techniques and either dismiss discussion altogether in favor of lecture or allow discussion to limp along in the hopes that it will improve. Writing during reading can help students and teachers establish effective discussions so we can then take a "backseat" while students actively take charge of their own learning.

Organizing a discussion poses challenges. Many of us bristle at the idea of putting a student on the spot, calling on him or her out of the blue and expecting an answer. Calling on an unprepared student often results in embarrassing the student and does nothing to facilitate class conversation. It may even make students who would participate retreat in fear of being similarly called out. At the very best, this "cold calling" can encourage a student to rattle off an unconsidered answer, which, again, does nothing to help warm up conversation.

We've discovered that starting with low-stakes discussion options can help combat this problem. If we check students' writing before beginning discussion, we have a clear sense of how far the conversation might develop and how to push students who are not adequately prepared. Having students use a journal (often a journal assignment done for homework) as a starting point has allowed for the structuring of successful low-stakes discussions in our classrooms. When discussions stem from writing in response, we can require all student voices to participate, because risk is minimal and students will be prepared to share. After we check homework (see the last section for journal assessment ideas), we call on students who have done the homework to do the warm-ups described in Figure 4.4. Once discussion is moving, we can ask all students to contribute and respond to each other's ideas. (Note: We have been guilty of purposely calling on a student who does not have the homework, with the intent of motivating the student to complete the homework the next day. But more often than not, this tactic simply embarrasses the student. We have found it is more effective to talk with a student one-on-one to clarify homework expectations and provide support if needed.)

One option for low-stakes writing that prepares students for sharing with larger groups is working first with a partner, then with the entire class. This type of sharing frees us from responding to journals every day while still creating time for students to receive feedback on their ideas. We have found it effective to sometimes allow students to choose their own partners and sometimes assign partners. In this way students have the comfort of working with friends at times but also hear new ideas from many students. Using discussion as a method for nudging students to work with new peers helps to build a community of shared ideas and scholarship. (See Chapter 5 for more on developing questions and a silent discussion strategy.)

Figure 4.4
CLASSROOM DISCUSSION STRATEGIES

SOLO STUDENT SHARING (WARM-UPS)

Have students choose their favorite insight from their journal, one to two sentences in length, and read it aloud.

Have students choose their favorite question from the journal, one to two sentences in length, and read it aloud.

Have students read aloud one quotation that they took from the text. We follow up by asking if they commented on what intrigued them about the quotation, or we ask other students if they quoted the same or similar material. Model for students how to make connections among multiple passages.

PAIR-SHARE, THEN GROUP SHARING

Ask students to trade journals with another student and highlight the idea in their partner's journal that they find most intriguing. Ask them to share this line from their partner's journal with the class. (This approach also allows for student rather than teacher feedback and, in our experience, often makes students even more accountable for their homework than if the teacher collects everything.)

Allow students to read each other's journals, write a response, and then share all or part of their response with the whole class.

FULL-CLASS DISCUSSIONS AND GRADED DISCUSSIONS

Conduct a Socratic seminar.

Facilitate discussions based on teacher-generated questions.

Hold discussions based on student-generated questions.

Have students make "graffiti" discussions, in which students pass a large piece of butcher paper from group to group or rotate from station to station discussing specific questions. They may answer questions posed by the teacher or write their own questions for discussion. As the paper is passed to a new group, that group adds new information, facts, and quotations in support of their ideas.

Have students create artwork that generates discussion. For example, ask students to draw, individually, a scene from their reading and then compare impressions of characters, setting, and so on.

ASSESSMENT AND FEEDBACK

Create discussion rubrics. We often ask students to help with this process. Pose this question to students: If discussing helps us understand our reading, how do we reward quiet students in discussion? How do we make assertive students accountable for listening to others?

Have students grade each other. (This is very helpful as informal feedback or as minimally graded work.)

Online Discussions

We must admit, we are still in our infancy in our exploration of the use of online discussions. We know some of our colleagues have also delved into using Wikibooks and blogs for literature response. We recognize that knowing our students and bringing their lives into the classroom must involve an acknowledgment of the time they spend online. According to a recent study conducted by the Kaiser Family Foundation, "The average young American now spends practically every waking minute—except for the time in school—using a smart phone, computer, television or other electronic device. . . . Those ages 8 to 18 spend more than seven and a half hours a day with such devices" (Rideout, Foehr, and Roberts 2010). We must learn to adjust our teaching accordingly while still being mindful that not all students have continuous access to electronic media. A wiki, or collaborative Web site, can provide a forum outside of the classroom for students to discuss their reading and share links, visuals, and videos related to the texts assigned. Blogs not only help students, teachers, and parents remain in touch outside of classroom time, but can provide a low-pressure alternative to formal written journals. Social networking sites, such as Ning (http://www.ning.com), allow students to pose questions and track responses online. All of these electronic media can be easily archived so that teachers and students have instant access to student model responses. (See Kajder 2007 in the References for more on technology that facilitates low-stakes writing.)

In an interview with a student who has been writing online forum postings as one of the requirements for her literature class, Kimberly learned that there were several advantages to the online approach. The student, Leah, reported that she liked the fact that everyone in the class had to post weekly responses. "This allowed the quiet people to be heard rather than drowned out by the loud voices that often take over class discussions." She also appreciated when the teacher invited students to do research to support their online postings. For example, Leah had to find an interesting fact about William Blake prior to the study of his poetry. The online forum allowed her to learn an interesting fact about Blake on her own and also learn facts from her classmates. And online forum posts are an example of low-stakes writing that can support more formal writing. Leah was asked to take one of her forum posts and develop it into an essay. Because she already had an idea and some quotes from the forum posting, she found it easier to get started. "I wasn't starting with a blank piece of paper; I already had a paragraph. I already had thought about it."

In addition to supporting students' own thinking and writing, reading other students' online forum posts can help to clarify or even introduce new ideas about the literature. It's a written discussion.

Some teachers provide questions to prompt online forum posting. Some teachers choose not to be part of the forum; others join in with their own posts, which allow students to be privy to the teacher's thinking and responses. This can be great modeling of the kinds of responses the teacher wants.

Requiring online forum posts also provides evidence that students are reading and provides evidence of students' thinking processes in response to their reading. This data can inform planning for follow-up discussions in class and for clarifications of the text, and can even identify students who may need some one-on-one attention to scaffold their understanding.

It's our hope that low-stakes writing and written or verbal discussion in response to literature teach students the importance of trusting their own thoughts and ideas. Journal writing often becomes drafts for the kinds of essays and responses we detail in Chapters 5, 6, and 7. We recognize that all of our students will not choose to be published authors, but we want them to discover what Brenda Ueland describes based on her years of teaching writing: "Everybody is talented, original, and has something important to say" ([1938] 1987, 3).

CHAPTER 5

WRITING TO EXPLORE

On a Thursday afternoon in early October, a junior asked, "Is there something between low-stakes writing and high-stakes writing?" It's an intriguing question—one we have been pondering in our own teaching and in writing this book. We checked in with colleagues, who spoke of creating "bridge assignments" between low-stakes and high-stakes, or what were more typically labeled as "formal" or "analytical" essays. Our colleagues described "expanded journal entries," "mini-essays," "focus essays," "question essays," "collaborative essays," and "personal vignettes in response to literature." As we talked about these bridge assignments, we were struck by teachers' use of the word *exploratory*.

We could see the possibilities of exploratory writing as a way for students to gain confidence in their ability to question and argue free from the constraints of *what they perceive to be* accomplished academic writing. (We develop these ideas further in Chapter 6, in which we discuss approaches to more formal thesis-driven or argument-driven writing.) We were delighted to discover that "exploratory writing" exists in the field of English education. In his book *The Literature Workshop*, Sheridan Blau offers this description of an exploratory essay: "[It is] one that does not so much advance an argument as examine and explore avenues for solving an interpretive or critical problem (e.g., an exploration of the problem of point of view and narrative evaluation in Alice Walker's 'Everyday Use')" (2003, 179). Blau notes that such an essay encourages students to "understand that a literary essay need not be more devoted to demonstrating the validity of a particular point of view than to illuminating and clarifying a sometimes uncertain and multidimensional reality" (180). We agree with this notion and have appreciated the opportunity to stretch ourselves to find ways to apply Blau's idea of exploratory essays as well as the other types of exploratory writing we discussed with our colleagues in the middle and high school classroom. What follows are our discoveries about how to help students make meaning from their reading and from their initial responses, and how to help them articulate questions and possible answers that will encourage them to wrestle with the complexities of literature rather than seek one correct "answer" to a text.

Exploratory writing strives primarily to make connections and showcase thinking, and inasmuch, may not be perfectly polished writing. Questioning a text and exploring possible answers to those questions is challenging for students, and is beneficial to them as writers and thinkers both in our classes and beyond. So, we need to allow space for this "messy" writing that honors students' development as thinkers and writers. Messy writing, though, requires a great deal from us as teachers.

We know that it does not work to tell a group of students, at any age, "Take a look through your journals and then write a thesis statement." This kind of instruction leads to many questions for the teacher, including, What should I be looking for in my journal? and What is a thesis statement? And then there are the under-the-surface questions, the questions we read on students' faces but they do not always know how to articulate: How does my journal lead to a thesis? Why should I argue about this story anyway? Students need to be actively taught to move from observation to question to claim. We know we need to allow students to develop these skills over time. Also, we know it is not possible to teach all of these skills over the course of just one unit of instruction. The writing proposed here will help students develop confidence in the value of exploring multiple interpretations and developing the ideas in their journals. Here students begin drawing connections among seemingly disparate observations in their reading and start to see an author's purpose more clearly. They use their writing to articulate those incipient thoughts rather than attempt to appear authoritative when they have not formed a clear interpretation. Ultimately, we hope they learn to trust their ability to think through the many layers of a complex text and to appreciate that there is no one ready "answer" waiting for them when they read challenging literature. In Chapter 2 we outlined the importance of using backward planning to structure a literature unit that includes writing. Exploratory writing is no different. When we ask students to write about a text, but do not require them to respond to specific teacher-generated questions or thesis statements, we must explicitly teach them how to question a text.

DEVELOPING QUESTIONS

Questioning by students, and our feedback on their questions, needs to be scheduled in to the unit so that students do not arrive at the end of the text unable to articulate their own questions. We encourage modeling multiple layers of questioning throughout the unit so that students develop the metacognition to determine the difference between a question that requires them to demonstrate comprehension and a question that demonstrates an awareness of deeper themes in the text.

In her book *Making the Journey*, Leila Christenbury (2006) has an excellent chapter, "The Craft of Questioning." We turn to this rich resource often for ideas for developing questions that move beyond comprehension and support students in connecting the text, their own experiences, and the world.

Teacher Ben Klash uses levels of questions to support his sophomore students in developing questions in response to the literature they are reading:

> *Level one questions* **are reading quiz questions (they focus on comprehension of the text).**
>
> *Level two questions* **are synthesis questions (they are rooted in the text but require students to dig deeper—to connect important aspects of the text: characters, setting, plot, themes, point of view, style, and tone).**
>
> *Level three questions* **are open-ended questions (they go beyond the text to connect with students' experiences, other texts, and the world).**

Ben provides multiple opportunities for his students to develop questions based on these levels. One of his effective strategies that weaves question development with individual and group work is silent discussion. We have detailed his strategy in Figure 5.1.

Figure 5.1

STRATEGY: SILENT DISCUSSIONS
Students work in small groups to frame questions based on the levels—one for each level. Each group has its questions checked by the teacher.
Questions are written on butcher paper sheets and posted in the classroom. Students circulate around the room in their small groups and respond to each of the other groups' questions.
Then each group gets its questions sheet back. They analyze each question and the responses from the silent discussion. The group decides on its best question and response, and then a group spokesperson presents the question and response to the whole class.
As each group presents their question/response, the discussion deepens. Students go beyond the original questions. They make links to other groups' questions, critique their questions as they talk, and see new connections to the text.
IDEAS FOR MODIFYING THIS STRATEGY
Questions are circulated on butcher paper among the groups for response rather than posted on the wall.
Students write individual answers to the questions on notebook paper first and then work together as a group to combine their responses.
Groups are assigned specific questions to answer rather than asked to respond to all of the questions.
The teacher models a sample question and response (Ben uses models he has kept from previous years) before students write their own questions and respond to others' questions.
ASSESSMENT AND FEEDBACK
Have students write exit notes in which they respond to two questions:
1. What did you notice about how your classmates responded to your group's questions?
2. What did you learn from today's discussion?

The discussion and exit notes described in Figure 5.1 provide Ben with data about students' understanding of developing questions and how they are interacting with each other about the text. He uses this data to further develop students' question-writing and discussion skills.

G. Douglas Meyers (2002) finds that students benefit from developing written questions to bring to a class discussion. In his work "Whose Inquiry Is It Anyway? Using Students' Questions in the Teaching of Literature," he lists a number of question-development activities. The key is that students are focused on generating their questions, not answering them. Meyers notes, "When students are not encumbered by the need to provide answers, their questions grow in importance, interest, and complexity" (62). We have used several of Meyers's strategies not just for class discussion but also in support of exploratory essays. In particular, we find that asking students to develop a "key question" that they believe is "important and thought-provoking" is a good place to begin (Meyers 2002, 62). We have also used Meyers's strategy of having students create a list of key questions and then rank-order them. And we have adapted one of Meyers's strategies of creating questions based on response categories in asking our students to develop a question based on our list of "Kinds of Responses" (see Chapter 2). For example, an eighth grader came up with the following questions about "form/craft" in response to Joan Bauer's "A Letter from the Fringe": *How does the author use fragments in her telling of this story? Is this choice effective?*

EXPLORATORY ESSAYS

Teaching question development is one important aspect of pushing students to explore, but we have learned to consider the timing of teaching an exploratory essay as well. Considering when to teach the exploratory essay is crucial. We have had some success using the process of exploratory writing as the first phase in teaching younger secondary students to learn about creating an argument. For example, in Kristi's freshman English class, she taught thesis writing as an exploration of the connection between character and theme. Students used their writing to clarify the connections they discovered rather than to write an argument. She sees this writing as a fine result for novice writers, but perhaps a step in the drafting phase for more advanced writers. When working with more advanced writers, the seniors in her IB English classes, Kristi has experimented with assigning an exploratory essay at the beginning of the year to help students determine their own definition of "effective" writing. This essay, in which students chose one poem from among fourteen taught to the class and then argued why it was the most effective, challenged students' definitions of what an essay should do. They were pushed to define strong writing for themselves and to find examples. This initial piece of writing helped students trust their own opinions and explore the nuances of a text rather than respond to a narrow, teacher-created topic.

In the remainder of this chapter, we detail a variety of approaches to exploratory writing. As noted at the start of this chapter, these explorations can be used as stand-alone assessments or as bridges between low-stakes writing and the more formal thesis-driven or argument-driven essays described in Chapter 6, or even bridges to the "Literature as Mentor" and "Literature as Inspiration" writing detailed in Chapter 7.

FORMAL JOURNAL ENTRIES

In Chapter 4, we outlined strategies for writing during reading. The "formal" journal entry asks students to develop an idea they have uncovered in their literature journal or even during class discussion and to expand the short response into a more formal short paper. (See Figure 5.2 for details on the assignment.) When completing this assignment, students must return to their initial impressions, make connections, and ask questions to deepen their thinking rather than write a complete argument. Kristi credits one of her college professors with this idea, and has seen it translated successfully to the high school classroom. The formal journal not only provides students with an avenue to develop their thoughts but also allows teachers to assess the depth of students' thoughts about a text.

MINI-ESSAYS

Teacher Ben Klash adapted Natalie Goldberg's "The Rules of Writing Practice" (1990) in developing this idea. He recognizes the importance of daily writing. For the mini-essay, students write for ten minutes. The primary goal is to follow Goldberg's advice: "keep your hand moving" (1990, 2). Students need to develop the habit of getting words on paper: their initial thoughts. Ben uses a variety of prompts in support of this effort, including questions based on the text and prompts related to personal narrative, and he has had great success using video clips from the Web site of the *New York Times* to prompt student writing. Each day his sophomores write for ten minutes, exploring a variety of topics. He notes that students are not restricted in how they respond: some write narratives, and others turn to fiction. The goal is two-fold: he wants students to develop a habit of writing, and he wants them to discover that they can think by putting pen to paper.

After several weeks of writing practice, Ben focuses his students on writing in response to literature they are reading. In his sophomore class, students write mini-essays in support of exploring *Antigone*. In these essays, they explore ideas from their reading and class discussions. Ben also provides prompts to nudge students' thinking. Again, the practice is daily; students generate a number of mini-essays. They then read their collection of mini-essays and select from them to craft a longer, polished essay.

Figure 5.2

STRATEGY: THE FORMAL JOURNAL ENTRY
Begin with students' literature notebooks. Ask them to read through their journals and class notes and find an interesting idea that they would like to explore. They might find, for example, a quotation that is worthy of analysis, a common idea running through several journal entries that needs to be clearly connected, or even a question they asked at the beginning of the text that they would now like to answer. Teachers will need to model this process with their own journals and notes so that they explicitly teach students the difference between exploring (developing) an idea and repeating what they have already written. (See Appendix D1, "Sample Formal Journal.") Note that formal journals can be assigned at any time during the reading of a text.
Ask students to type a one-page formal journal that addresses the topic they have chosen. The journal may take the form of a stream-of-consciousness discussion, a list of questions, or even the beginning of an analysis that incorporates textual evidence in support of one clear topic.
IDEAS FOR MODIFYING THIS STRATEGY
Require a specific number of quotations or amount of support.
Allow students to work with partners or small groups to find connections among their journals and then write one collaborative formal journal.
Structure the formal journal as an in-class, on-demand essay. Provide class time for students to look through their journals and develop a response. This works well as a comprehension check and allows teachers to determine the depth of students' analyses, as students' focus remains on content rather than essay formatting.
ASSESSMENT AND FEEDBACK
Collect and comment on journals. Streamline grading by limiting length (we recommend no more than one page) and/or asking students to highlight their most important question or observation for a response.
Ask students to comment on each other's formal journals.

Teacher Marisa Real also uses mini-essays in support of students exploring Eric Schlosser's book *Fast Food Nation*. She provides questions for each section of the book. Students select a question and respond in a mini-essay that incorporates the question and includes supporting quotes. An example of a question from one section of the book is as follows: According to Schlosser, what are some of the methods advertisers use to learn about children's tastes? Do you think these methods are ethical? Why or why not? After writing several mini-essays, Marisa provides students with another set of questions from which they choose to develop a longer essay. These questions allow students to build on the work they did in their mini-essays. For example, this question for a longer essay connects with one of the earlier mini-essay questions:

> Over the last several decades, fast-food companies have aggressively targeted children in their marketing efforts. Should advertisers be permitted to target children, who may lack the sophistication to make informed decisions and are essentially being lured into eating high-fat, high-calorie food through toys and cute corporate mascots? Is it possible that fast-food companies—like tobacco companies—are recruiting increasingly younger consumers in order to ensure a steady customer base as their older constituents die from heart disease, diabetes, and other obesity-related disorders?

Again, the task for students is to incorporate the question, supporting quotes from Schlosser's text, and the thinking and writing they have done in their mini-essays.

FOCUS ESSAYS

The focus essay builds on the idea of mini-essays by keeping the length and focus of the essay narrow. We appreciate how it can be used to support student interest and voice. Students are asked to explore an aspect of a text: point of view, a character, the setting, and/or symbols. Drawing on the work of Pearl Amelia McHaney (2004) in her article about focus essays for *English Journal*, we recommend that students begin their focus essays with a quote from the text. They then "focus" their attention on how this quote illustrates the aspect of the text they are exploring. The result is a short analysis of one aspect of a text that not only informs the student-author but also can be shared with the class as part of an examination of the author's craft in a particular text. For example, students might explore the significance of the title, the use of similes, the role of dialogue, the impact of repetition, or the use of a motif.

We have seen classrooms where focus essays are written at the very beginning of a text study. Students read the text and develop a focus essay prior to the in-class analysis and discussion of the text. Teachers might also have students read the first chapter or two of a novel and then develop a focus to explore through a focus essay. These essays can then be used throughout the unit of study to highlight and illustrate the content and craft of the text. Kristi assigns "key passage" essays that direct students to find one key passage and explore its implications for characterization, theme, or another literary element. Such essays build directly on the focus that a student may have written about during reading, or on a passage jotted down in his or her journal (See Chapter 4 for more on literature journals.)

QUESTION ESSAYS

The question essay builds on the importance of developing questions described in the earlier section of this chapter (see page 80). As Meyers writes in his article about the importance of student-generated questions, "[E]ach reader of each work of literature, as Langer notes, is 'reaching toward a horizon of possibilities,' possibilities of understanding which cohere and develop as 'envisionments'—unique sets of ideas, images, and questions about the literary work" (Meyers 2002, 61–62, quoting Langer 1992, 37–39).

Although this question essay can take on a variety of structures, at its heart is the opportunity for students to develop a question or questions about a text and then explore their questions—not for the purpose of developing a single answer but rather to honor the "wondering."

A question essay can be a series of questions with possible answers. This can take the form of a dialogue between the student-writer and the text.

A question essay can also be a series of questions with possible answers that ends in the development of a "key question." In some cases, the key question can then be written about in a subsequent essay. We have also found value in using the key questions developed by students as the basis for a class discussion rather than for an additional essay.

And we have seen question essays that are explorations of a single question about a text, but in which the focus is on possible answers, not a single answer. Students provide examples and quotes from the text in support of their answers. As Blau notes in encouraging this exploratory approach by students,

> I want them to abandon the thesis-argument essay, . . . insofar as they believe that the form requires them to prove a particular point of view over others when their own understanding of a story or issue might be richly illuminated by recognizing and affirming the value of multiple perspectives or uncertainty about any stable or single position as a correct one. (2003, 180)

Students have explored the following questions, with no single answer:

- In the novel *Pride and Prejudice*, which character represents which trait? Is Elizabeth pride or prejudice? What about Mr. Darcy?

+ Did Gene intend to bounce the tree limb in *A Separate Peace*? Or was it a tragic accident?
+ In the play *Romeo and Juliet*, what do we know about the relationship of Juliet's parents? How does their relationship influence Juliet?
+ How does the culture in *Fahrenheit 451* compare with our current culture? In what ways are we becoming like them? In what ways are we different?

Teacher Colin Pierce invited the sophomores in his honors English class to develop a personal commentary in response to a question each student developed about the text *To Kill a Mockingbird*. Students could use a question they had already asked in their journal writing or one that came out of class discussions. Once students identified their question, they were to list key passages from the text and from their literature journal that addressed the question as well as their plan for exploring their question in writing. (See Appendix D2 for Colin Pierce's original "Journal Assignment" and Appendix D3 for his subsequent "Personal Commentary Question Proposal" assignment.) Students' questions included these:

+ What is the relevance of the title in *To Kill a Mockingbird*?
+ What is Boo Radley afraid of? Why doesn't he come out of his house?
+ How has the influence of the adults and the surrounding community affected Jem and Scout? How will it affect them later on?
+ What is the significance of Mrs. Dubose?
+ What does the book say about bravery?

COLLABORATIVE ESSAYS

We concur with Sheridan Blau's recognition that providing time and practice for group work in support of learning about literature "contributes to the construction of a particular kind of classroom community and classroom culture and for the sort of ethos it fosters for intellectual work within such a culture" (2003, 56).

In this section we describe our experiences with the collaborative essay, which we first learned about when Kimberly was working with a group of juniors to read and understand Thoreau's *Walden*. These students had been reading excerpts from *Walden* and writing in response to the excerpts in their literature journals. They had been sharing their journal writing throughout the unit and on the day we'll describe, they were brainstorming topics that they would like to explore in an essay about *Walden*. A student named Susan noted, "It is so helpful to hear the quotes from other students. I wish I had all of these to use in my essay." Aha!

When the class came back from their small-group work, Kimberly asked Susan to share her comment with the whole group. Heads nodded in agreement, which encouraged Kimberly to propose that the class try writing a collaborative essay. Students were willing to give this new approach a try. The next step was to form groups based on topics. This took longer than anticipated, but after putting topics on the board and facilitating some lobbying for additional topics, groups of three or four were formed. The class then negotiated individual responsibilities: each student would write a draft introduction for the topic and one supporting paragraph with quotes, using their literature journals and the text. Students agreed that to be part of a collaborative essay group, they would have to bring in the agreed-upon drafts. If not, they were on their own for this essay. And the students came through—each with a draft in hand. (Kimberly chose to see this as an embrace of the collaborative approach rather than as avoidance of writing an individual essay.)

Over the next two days, students collaborated, using the best parts of their draft introductions and, in the case of one group, writing a new introduction. Supporting paragraphs were then revised and organized collaboratively by the group. Conclusion paragraph drafts were assigned as homework—by the students—and they used these drafts the next day to craft a group conclusion. As students collaborated, Kimberly witnessed engaged—even heated—debates about word choice, sentence structure, whether the comma goes inside the quotation marks, and which quotes to use. In a number of cases, students went back to the text in search of further clarification.

Putting the final draft together was a challenge. Some of the perfectionists in the class wanted to take all the paragraphs home and rewrite them into one cohesive essay. But others thought this wasn't fair, because it required too much work for one group member. And some members of one group met with Kimberly privately about their concern that the volunteer scribe would make additional changes not agreed upon by the group. So the compromise was to use class time to write the paragraphs into one essay. Most groups finalized their supporting paragraphs individually and then cut and pasted them onto blank sheets of paper with the collaboratively written introductions and conclusions.

As she sat down over the weekend to read their collaborations, Kimberly was struck by how the lively conversations she had witnessed had led to thoughtful, voice-filled essays. The introductions and conclusions were some of the best she had read from this group. And although there were awkward transitions between the supporting paragraphs that were written by separate individuals, she could see how students who struggled with quote analysis had benefited from working with classmates. The supporting paragraphs had evidence and explanation. An added bonus is that she had nine essays to read instead of thirty-three.

We want to be candid in saying that collaborative essays are time consuming. A key component is to build in individual accountability to ensure that each student is contributing and to allow for the assessment of individual student understanding. Typically we do a collaborative essay once or twice a year. But it's been our experience that the time and structure needed are worth the rich conversations that this approach to writing fosters. As Blau describes, "Students get to work with one another . . . [in a way that] they are able to do more together than any of them can do by themselves, and through that process grow toward greater autonomy and independence" (Blau 2003, 56).

There are numerous possibilities for adapting the collaborative essay. We have seen it used with a middle school class debate about *A Separate Peace* in which students were assigned sides and were required to frame a thesis and find supporting textual evidence regarding whether Gene's bouncing of the tree limb, which caused Finny to fall, was intentional or accidental. Students then collaborated to write an essay in support of their "side," using the debate evidence as their rough draft. These essays could also be an individual assignment.

In his book *The Literature Workshop*, Sheridan Blau (2003) describes a two-stage interpretation project that incorporates collaborative writing. This project requires students to write an interpretative paper on a poem or short story (Blau provides them with a list of works, which he describes as challenging, from which to choose). For the first stage, students draw on their own reading to write an essay, and are expected to incorporate library or Web-based research as well. Students then meet with others who are writing about the same poem or short story and share their papers. For stage 2 of the project, students revise their individual paper, with the requirement that they "draw upon one or more of the papers written by [their] colleagues to support, clarify, or stand in contrast to [their] own ideas about the text" (2003, 177).

Jim Burke's description of group essay options in *The English Teacher's Companion* (2003, 168–170) is a helpful resource.

We have also seen students work together in pairs to coauthor an essay. Again, each student is given specific tasks to complete, and then they come together to create a final product. We can tout the benefits of such collaboration based on our work to coauthor this book. We are grateful for how our conversations deepened our understanding and provided a sounding board for revision and editing ideas.

PERSONAL VIGNETTE/TEXT-TO-SELF CONNECTIONS ESSAYS

"Write about an experience with literature that turned your head around." This invitation from Tom Romano happened at a workshop hosted by Lewis & Clark College, which Kimberly attended along with graduates who were participating in a

new teacher seminar. To respond to the prompt, participants were invited to make
a map of their relationship with literature, noting positive and negative experiences
in their reading history. Kimberly wrote about her joy while reading Marge Piercy's
poetry for the first time and discovering *Our Town* in her first year of teaching junior
English. And she remembered the sheer boredom she felt as her high school English
teacher read *Julius Caesar* aloud. Even his British accent was not enough to hold her
attention. Tom Romano's workshop was designed to help us, as teachers, rediscover
our own writing voice with the hope that we would create classrooms that supported
our students' writing voice. We were privileged to try many of the writing invitations
described in Romano's book *Crafting Authentic Voice* (2004).

Our own exploration of literature relationships served as a reminder that personal
connections with literature can be powerful—that there is a place for narrative and
"I" in responses to literature. In his chapter "The Five-Paragraph You-Know-What,"
Romano quotes Nancy Sommers's essay about the role of the personal in college
academic writing:

> **Being personal, I want to show my students, does not mean being
> autobiographical. Being academic does not mean being remote, distant,
> imponderable. Being personal means bringing their judgment and
> interpretation to bear on what they read and write, learning that they
> never leave themselves behind even when they write academic essays.
> (2004, 66)**

Offering students the opportunity to explore their thinking can work as a precursor
to the formal analytical writing outlined in Chapter 6, or exploration of thinking can
stand on its own as an assessment of a student's understanding of a text. What we
wish to emphasize is the importance of prioritizing student thinking about a text over
adhering to traditional forms. We strive to find room in our curriculum over the year
or semester to offer a variety of essay structures, and we hope that exploratory options
allow students to push their thoughts and to view our classrooms as safe places to take
intellectual risks in their writing. The written responses outlined in Chapters 5, 6, and
7 do overlap from time to time, and we find that it is important to acknowledge this
overlap to students. For what do we, as writers, attempt on the way to a final product?
We write in response to a text, review our responses, write some more, explore essay
structures, and repeat—not necessarily in that order. Our students need to understand
that they can, and should, follow the same nonlinear process as they develop a written
response to literature.

Stephen Kramer, author and fourth-grade teacher, writes about letting go of formula or, in his words, "training wheels":

> **In the best writing—writing that makes you want to grab whoever's nearby and say, "Here read this!"—the trails lead to unexpected and delightful places. Voice, ideas, and organization work together in ways that are peculiar to the writer and the topic. Information and presentation combine in ways that couldn't possibly be predicted by any formula. The writing sings, and the reader senses that this is just the way the story needs to be told.**

We acknowledge that providing the time needed to support students' exploratory writing can be challenging. In this age of accountability and test prep, this time when teachers are continuously asked to do more with less, we are even more committed to hollowing out a space in our classroom to teach real thinking, even when it is nonstructured or inconclusive. We need to push students to use their writing as a way to develop their thinking, ask questions, and not settle for easy answers. We realize that we are placing yet another demand on ourselves and our overtaxed colleagues, because teaching writing in the ways outlined in this chapter requires us to work with students in small groups and one-on-one, and many of us have very large classes (see the discussion in Chapter 6 about conferencing with students). But this kind of coaching as students write is imperative.

Assessment can prove challenging when we assign exploratory writing. We will need to look at our grading practices and rethink how specific writing "traits" or other mandates can be demonstrated in exploratory writing. But in spite of the challenges they pose, the exploratory processes detailed in this chapter are invaluable building blocks for young writers. And we have found that students' exploratory writing is some of the most interesting work we read as teachers.

CHAPTER 6

WRITING AS AN AUTHORITY

According to Carol Jago, "The best method for helping students learn how to interpret and criticize literature is through writing" (2009, 3). We concur. But in her recent report, "Crash! The Currency Crisis in American Culture," she argues, "If the product, a 700–1,000 word essay on Maxine Hong Kingston's *Woman Warrior*, seems artificial and school-based, so be it. The intellectual process that students have employed to compose the paper is genuine" (2009, 3). We support Jago's regard for the intellectual process, but we respectfully suggest that the essays created should be in keeping with "that flexible rhetorical form whose roots go back at least to Michel de Montaigne" (Romano 2004, 61). We embrace James Moffett's view of essays:

> **Through the essays of Swift, Lamb, Hazlitt, and DeQuincey to those of Orwell, Virginia Woolf, Joan Didion, and Norman Mailer, English literature has maintained a marvelous tradition, fusing personal experience, private vision, and downright eccentricity, with intellectual rigor and verbal objectification. In color, depth, and stylistic originality it rivals some of our best poetry. (Moffett 1983, 171)**

This expansive view of essays is aligned with research that challenges a heavy reliance on the five-paragraph formula for essays (see Chapter 1). We share the concerns raised in this research about how reliance on formula limits students' thinking and focuses their attention primarily on the structure of their essay rather than on what message they are trying to convey. As George Hillocks notes, "Formula not only fails to 'support higher level thinking skills' but actually imposes 'a way of thinking that eliminates the need for critical thought' (Spandel 2005, 125, quoting Hillocks 2002, 136). We want students to write essays that demonstrate their close reading of text, that show their ability to use evidence from the text in support of exploration and/or argument, and that reflect their original thinking.

We call for an approach to essay writing that builds on the reading and discussion activities described in Chapters 3, 4, and 5. These activities require students to think about the literature in a way that scaffolds the writing of their analytical responses. We also call for the use of real-world models for writing about literature. As noted in Chapter 1, students need to read and analyze essays so that they have a model for what they are writing. In Chapter 5 we recommend collaborative writing, which provides an opportunity for students to develop ideas and then reflect and revise their thinking in conversations with fellow writers. We also discuss "bridge" assignments, which ask students to build on their initial writing and thinking by developing ideas through focused writing. In this chapter we support students in learning to write with purpose and authority in an organized, analytical essay free of formula.

At the heart of good essay writing, like all writing, is content development. Students need to know what they are trying to say. Throughout the chapter we stress the importance of writing process—focusing on students as they write, helping them organize the evidence that they have gathered, and using that evidence to articulate their opinions about texts. We discuss the importance of mini-lessons that enhance writing craft and combat common errors, and we will touch on the importance (and difficulties, given our class sizes) of conferencing with students and providing structured peer response opportunities.

APPROACHING ESSAYS AS A THOUGHT PROCESS RATHER THAN A FORMULA

Most English/language arts curricula require teachers to teach students to analyze literature. Increasingly, students are asked to write expository essays at the middle school level, and many teachers may choose to approach that requirement with literary analysis. Writing critically about a text poses many challenges to adolescents, but is invaluable in helping them develop their intellects. As Purves, Rogers, and Soter note,

> Such writing moves students from the concrete to the abstract and, consequently, fosters the development of analogical reasoning skills.
>
> Such writing requires students to focus on text rather than self and, therefore, promotes the development of an objective stance that paves the way for critical appreciation of the *qualities* of the literature, even though students may not personally like certain aspects of the literary work (e.g. its conclusion or one or more characters).
>
> Such writing helps students develop generalizing and reasoning skills that, at later stages, enable them to link together other books and issues and, therefore, broaden the scope of literary appreciation. (1995, 168)

Teaching literary analysis, then, has far-reaching effects on our students' academic and personal growth. Yet we acknowledge the challenge of helping students move "from the concrete to the abstract" and still write something that enables us to comprehend their thought process. We want to help them structure the ideas that arise while they read without reliance on the five-paragraph formula that dominates so many secondary classrooms. Many of us were taught (or actively teach) the classic five-paragraph essay format: introductory paragraph with a lead, context, and thesis at the end of it, then three paragraphs with clear topic sentences and supporting details, and finally a conclusion that restates the thesis and introduction. It has become commonplace to assume that this is the most sound way to analyze literature, and the best approach for beginners.

Structure has its place, to be sure, and students need to know how to communicate complex and confusing ideas, how to defend a thesis, and how to show, in an organized and coherent way, that they have gathered evidence to support their claims. However, our years of teaching and reading essays confirm the research we discuss in Chapter 1. We have found that students can use the formula to say very little in a very organized way. When students attempt to "fit" an argument into an established or required form, they prioritize form over content. This results in the following dominant flaws in the five-paragraph essays that we have read (note that teachers' and students' intellects are undermined in this process):

1. *Students create an argument prematurely and write a mediocre (at best) paper to support a thesis that they came up with before they worked through the process of evaluating and analyzing evidence. Essentially, they try to make evidence fit an idea they have, rather than surveying the evidence they have gathered to discover what it tells them. Consequently, they often quote out of context or attempt to make a text do something it is not really doing. As a colleague notes, "The text gets in the way of their argument."*

2. *Thesis statements are used that the students themselves do not understand, but that they have crafted to include three key points.*

3. *"Fancy organizing" of obvious facts from the text is done rather than an exploration of the student's own response to the text. For example, an exploration of setting in a short story simply becomes a list of three quotations in which the author describes the setting, without students including comments on the importance of those moments or including their thoughts on why the setting functions as it does.*

4. *Bland conclusions are written that do nothing to leave a reader thinking or solidify an argument.*

5.   *Teachers, either directly or indirectly, guide students to restate the teacher's opinions in a tidy, easy-to-grade structure. Thus teachers implicitly encourage a lazy reading process and a lazy writing process.*

6.   *Students genuinely struggle to express their argument (or assume their argument is wrong) when they have found two or four (or more) supporting pieces of evidence, rather than the mandated number of three.*

Students *want* to learn to express sophisticated ideas in an engaging format, but we end up leading them to hollow arguments by prioritizing structure over personal responses to the text, and by discouraging independent research that follows the students' own passions rather than ours.

With a wink to the traditional beginning, middle, and end formula of writing, we have organized this chapter with a discussion of gathering evidence first, *then* writing a thesis, then determining how to conclude. Note: the emphasis is on evidence gathering before the topic is selected. This supports our belief that students need to have ideas and questions about the text, and some material on which to comment, *before* they can clearly state their argument. As one of our colleagues notes, a paper should have a clear purpose, but that thesis might not be stated until it is proven—it may need to come in the conclusion. A student's thought process should determine the form, and not the other way around.

Outlining our own teaching units often looks something like the following list, so our chapter follows a similar format. But again, in the true spirit of doing the work of thinking through our own structure as teachers and writers, we frequently experiment when designing units. We change the order of the steps, add or subtract steps, and make the process our (and our students') own. Please also note that the following list has helped us structure the teaching of a lengthy analytical essay over the course of several weeks, but we have had success teaching parts of this process with analytical paragraphs and short (one-page) essays to younger students, and with giving feedback to struggling students by assigning a due date to each individual step.

Read the text, using close-reading strategies outlined in Chapter 3 and during-reading, low-stakes writing strategies outlined in Chapter 4.

Review evidence from journals, discussion notes, and other in-class and homework writings.

Choose a topic.

Highlight/tab support and connections in journals, notes, and other writings.

Articulate a question that might lead to a thesis (see Chapter 5 for ideas on question development).

Outline and/or draft a response to the question. Lessons to consider include the following:

> Incorporating evidence
> Writing a thesis
> Writing a conclusion

Ensure that the thesis and the evidence connect. If not, redraft one or both.

 Mini-lessons on structure and craft for revision (taught according to the goals of your unit plan)

Peer/teacher conferences (can be done at any point in the process)

Finalize the draft.

GATHERING AND ANALYZING TEXTUAL EVIDENCE

What if students have few ideas and nowhere to begin once the essay is assigned? This is unlikely, if we have assisted them in reading and writing along the way. As we outlined in our earlier chapters, helping students write in response as they read will help them to find something they want to say about a book. Having read their thoughts and collected some low-stakes writing, we can conference with students on the path to a final essay and help them use their writing to guide topic choice and evidence. Their literature journal responses, or "impressionistic responses" in the words of Purves, Rogers and Soter (1995), become scaffolding for analytical pieces. We have seen proof of Purves, Rogers, and Soter's (1995) argument that "analytic writing does not mean . . . that exploratory writing and revision disappear. After the initial impressionistic responses are recorded in language and forms familiar to the student, teachers and students may select from these pieces those that suggest further possibilities and that may be reworked to move toward a more objective discussion of the literary text" (164).

Compiling evidence and asking questions along the way also helps students avoid the last-minute panic that can result in plagiarism. In fact, structured journals can push students to gather evidence as they read and will keep them from simply repeating arguments they've heard in class. For example, in our sample unit plan for *Chronicle of a Death Foretold* (see Appendix A3), we ask students to respond to key quotations in each night's reading in their journals. The final assignment, a key passage essay, might already be drafted in their journal when they reach the end of the book. Or, they may choose another passage to respond to but use the evidence they have gathered in their journal as support. Once a student has been guided to *think* about and *question* a text, he or she has many possibilities for writing a final product. We find it invaluable to model this process for students with our own journal, and for students to share ideas with each other in pairs and small groups (see the section titled "In-Class Conferencing" in this chapter).

As we guide students to their discovery of a topic, we keep in mind the "Kinds of Responses" outlined in Chapter 2, which we have used to guide the construction of the unit plan. If we plan to push students to discuss form and craft in the text, for example, we will help them comb through their journals and in-class writing to find the moments when they comment most saliently on the effect of a certain literary technique. Then we can help them trace any pattern and connections in the journal and lead them back to key parts of the text to aid in developing their argument.

When students have chosen a topic and begun writing, it is essential to teach mini-lessons on using evidence, and to show students what effective analysis of evidence looks like (see, for example, Figures 6.1 and 6.2). Students need to know how to integrate quotations by using their own thoughts and analyses to introduce and comment on the writer's words, and they need us to provide explicit modeling of the difference between restating a quotation and commenting on a quotation. In their book *Writing About Literature*, Johannessen, Kahn, and Walter emphasize the importance of teaching a vocabulary for analysis:

> The *claim* is the conclusion (or generalization) that is advanced; the *data* are the evidence or the specific details presented in support of the conclusion; and the *warrant* is the explanation of why the data justify the claim or, in other words, authorization for the "leap" from the data to the claim. (2009, 12)

They explain that students must be taught "how to select and use appropriate evidence" to avoid "extended summary" (Johannessen, Kahn, and Walter 2009, 12–13). We concur, and we use their recommendations to guide us in crafting lesson plans to teach analysis.

Although we often use our own writing to model the difference between summarizing and analyzing, it is enormously helpful to keep student models and use them from year to year. This enables us to use one specific paragraph in a student essay as a model rather than handing out an entire model essay to read. We also gather examples from different student writers so that students can see that there is no one "right" style when it comes to analysis.

Figure 6.1 outlines a strategy for using in-class writing to teach that incorporating evidence into a literary analysis is a three-step process: introducing a quotation, quoting the text, and analyzing evidence from the text. This strategy has worked in our classes as a starting point. Figure 6.2 outlines a strategy that we use to follow up our initial in-class writing: showing students a model and asking them to determine what makes it a model, and then encouraging them to revise their own writing so that it more closely reflects the model.

Figure 6.1

STRATEGY: USING IN-CLASS FREE-WRITES AS DRAFTS TO TEACH INCORPORATING EVIDENCE
Begin with an in-class writing prompt and ask students to find one quotation from the text to support their response. For example, a prompt that asks students to explore the complications of friendship in John Steinbeck's *Of Mice and Men* might be supported with dialogue showing George's frequent frustration with Lennie. Have students write the supporting quotation they find at the top of a page, then write a response. At this stage, the response may not address the quotation directly. We want students to respond naturally, so that we can guide them from initial response to an analysis that clearly references evidence from the text.
After the writing is finished, begin a mini-lesson (see Appendix E1, "Incorporating Quotation Practice") showing students how to incorporate evidence by providing context and how to analyze evidence using their own response. Because they have already responded to the text, they should be ready to form or to develop an opinion.
IDEAS FOR MODIFYING THIS STRATEGY
Repeat the lesson the next day, requiring students to find another quotation in the text to support their argument. They will now have at least two pieces of evidence. Ask them to incorporate the evidence into the previous day's draft by introducing it clearly and analyzing it. Make this a routine writing expectation.
Give students a quotation already introduced (i.e., explained with context; again, see Appendix E1) and have them write the analysis. Or, give them quotations with analyses and have them write the context. This assignment works well as individual or partner practice.
Ask students to revise faulty examples.
ASSESSMENT AND FEEDBACK
Collect and comment on free-writes. Streamline grading by commenting only on the skill taught: introducing a quotation, quoting the text, or analyzing the quotation.
After having them practice for a few days, ask students to comment on each other's introductions and analyses.
If assigning an essay at the end of the unit, make sure there is a category on the essay rubric that specifically requires students to incorporate quotations gracefully.

Figure 6.2

STRATEGY: USING STUDENT MODELS TO TEACH INCORPORATING EVIDENCE
From a previous essay assignment, collect student models that show effective incorporation of textual evidence. Note that reproducing one paragraph incorporating evidence is more useful here than reproducing a whole essay, as it helps students to focus on one specific skill. See Appendix E2, "Student Model of Quotation Analysis," for an excerpt of a student's analysis of *Things Fall Apart* by Chinua Achebe.   Photocopy the student models (we find it helpful to photocopy graded essays, with students' names removed but our comments included so that students can see our responses) and give the models to students. Ask them to note what the student writers did that worked well. Ask, How did the student writers use their own words to introduce and analyze the quotation? Note: if you do not have a student model available, you may write one yourself.
IDEAS FOR MODIFYING THIS STRATEGY   Include the thesis with the analysis model, so that students can see how one short section of analysis supports a larger argument.   Give students the analyzed quotation and ask them to speculate about the thesis. Ask, How clearly does the writer articulate his or her point? Does he or she stay focused?   Write an example of a weak model (we avoid using student writing for this activity, as it unfairly singles students out, even when done anonymously) and ask students to improve it after they have reviewed a more effective model.   Write or collect several examples, ranging from weak to strong, and ask students to evaluate all of the examples, noting where weak examples can be improved and why strong examples work well.   Provide students with a rubric that specifically addresses quotation use. Have them evaluate the examples using the rubric, then apply that same rubric to their own writing.
ASSESSMENT AND FEEDBACK   Conduct a class discussion on the effectiveness of the writing in a model.   Assign final essays that will be evaluated for quotation integration and analysis.

TAKING A STAND: DISCOVERING AN ARGUMENT AND ARTICULATING A THESIS

Teaching students to argue and, ultimately, to write a thesis is crucial, but they need to have read the text with attention to detail and curiosity before they can formulate questions and opinions about the author's purpose. Students cannot write a thesis if we have not *actively taught* the text, and by this we mean structuring responses and journals along the way, guiding but not mandating students' thoughts in a discussion format (see Chapters 3, 4, and 5). Students need to be allowed to wrestle with their questions and try to find the answers to their questions in the text *before* they try to fit their writing into a form. Otherwise, they become convinced that the "answers" to their question are in the text somewhere and simply need to be hunted down and quoted in a prescribed format. See our discussion of essential and unit questions in Chapter 2 for help with framing a unit that continuously asks both teacher and student to approach the text with a purpose in mind, while still respecting individual responses to the text.

If we neglect to frame the unit, we end up teaching the thesis statement in the same way that we learned the thesis statement. We remember the one vague but unquestionable command: the thesis must be arguable. This is true, but what does it mean? And how do we get a student to question the text and not simply share a blasé opinion about the text and justify that as a thesis by saying, "It's arguable"? Traditionally we teach students to read the text, then craft a thesis statement, then go back and reread key sections of the text to support the position they have adopted. This approach asks students to value the form of an argument over their individual reactions to the text. Instead, we should emphasize true engagement with a text, questioning the text, and allowing that questioning to eventually lead to a thesis.

Teaching Thesis Statements Through Modeling

Kristi's first full realization that students were prioritizing structure over process (and that she had inadvertently encouraged it) came a few years ago, when she asked seniors to write an analytical essay on *The Awakening* by Kate Chopin. Students had written journals as they read, participated in graded and nongraded discussions, and done creative classroom activities to get at the heart of the text, and Kristi had allowed students the freedom to explore their own reactions. Still, many papers came in claiming that, ultimately, author Kate Chopin described her character Edna's awakening to us so that we too could find the independence that leads to happiness. Kristi was baffled. She had discussed the ending of the novel at length; how could students have mistaken the ending, Edna's probable suicide, as the result of her newfound happiness? Upon reviewing thesis statements and essay structure, however, she realized that students, keen to tie a motif in the text to the "author's message," knew how to write a tidy thesis that ended in a guide to finding happiness. Why else would Edna leave her husband, have an affair, and become an artist? Their desire to quickly round up three quotations that included their assigned motif, place the quotations into three body paragraphs, and sum it all up in the conclusion had led them to ignore what the quotations actually said. And, to be fair, their ability as adolescents to communicate the abstract ideas in the text in a way that did justice to the argument of the text was limited. They needed a teacher to guide them.

As Kristi explored her role in leading students to these erroneous conclusions, she realized that she and her department colleagues had been using a formula for thesis writing that they had learned several years earlier: What + How = Effect. This translates roughly to *what* the writer is doing (exploring the ramifications of a woman's defiance of traditional roles), *how* she is doing it (by contrasting Edna Pontellier with Madame Ratignolle), and what the *effect* is of her choices (we learn that independence can cost a woman her life). This pattern seemed to work, until Kristi noticed that students started creating what she calls the "Hallmark card thesis." They followed the pattern, but continuously arrived at the effect that the writer wants us all to be happy, or that the writer wants us to take risks or find ourselves, and so on. In short, they wanted writers to give us advice, and they wanted to prove it using three examples from the text.

Kristi worried that as she inadvertently taught the Hallmark card thesis, she encouraged students to ignore the complexity of the novel (and indeed the complexity of their own understanding of the novel) in favor of fitting one form for a universal thesis argument. Such essays can be easily downloaded or paraphrased from hundreds of Web sites, and the worst part is that they do not really require students to pose and answer their own questions. The only process students undergo is using a big, hard-to-define concept ("happiness") and trying to pin it to a character in a certain essay form. They do not get to pull apart the deeper meaning of a specific scene that captivated them, for example, because they are worried that there won't be "enough" to write about to fill all of their paragraphs or make their thesis "deep." And students do not ask, for example, what "happiness" might mean for a specific character, because an exploration of that would completely derail the form.

In an attempt to address the thesis conundrum, Kristi met with two colleagues. They compared notes on how they taught thesis statements and realized they needed to write their own thesis statements and share both the statements and their thinking process with their students. As they wrote, all three teachers realized they had been away from their undergraduate experiences long enough that they had forgotten their own analytical writing processes. Instead, they had absorbed the ways that the textbooks wanted them to argue and to teach argumentation. After brainstorming novels and poems as subjects for their project, they decided to keep the text simple and accessible: they watched an episode of *House* and drafted arguments. The three of them came up with very different statements. All were "deep" enough, all were arguable, all were sophisticated, but none of them followed a formula other than the desire of the writers to pinpoint and explain a complex thought. Students enjoyed seeing their teachers' personalities in their process and product and related to their efficiency, or, in Kristi's case, her lack of efficiency. She was able to talk with her students about the fact that she has always agonized over thesis statements, so she drafts and drafts and drafts again. But, once she has a thesis, it essentially maps out her paper and she can begin writing. Her colleague Jennifer Wecker, in contrast, produced multiple workable thesis statements so that she could choose the one that seemed most interesting for writing. Kristi could see the lightbulb go on over students' heads. She had not read a textbook that explained a thesis in these terms; it took talking with her peers and evaluating her own writing process to communicate with students how to approach a solid argument.

This exercise helped clarify for Kristi why her colleague Lori Townzen uses the term "thesis-driven essay" rather than "five-paragraph essay." The argument determines the length of the essay rather than the other way around. And it falls to us as teachers to help students determine what makes an argument "long enough" or "deep enough." Model essays can help with this. Asking students, "What is this essayist's argument and how does he or she organize the evidence?" teaches students to read nonfiction and teaches them to approach an essay as an attempt to explain their own ideas rather than fit a formula.

As students move toward writing their own nonformulaic arguments, we find it helpful to ask them to write out their ideas for a thesis as they read. Crafting an argument during reading gives students a focus and enables them to make connections from chapter to chapter. Also, students can have the challenging experience of the text disproving their initial ideas, prompting them to revise their ideas and find new evidence to support a new argument. In Figures 6.3, 6.4, and 6.5, we outline strategies to help students write and revise thoughtful thesis statements.

CONCLUDING THE ESSAY: WHY HAVE YOU ARGUED WHAT YOU HAVE ARGUED, AND WHY SHOULD YOUR READERS CARE?

One of the most immutable aspects of formulaic essay writing is the conclusion that simply rephrases the introduction. A colleague describes this as the "Tell 'em what you're going to say, say it, and then tell 'em what you said" style of writing. The conclusion, however, can and should be considered a dynamic component of the essay, a place to surprise or shock readers, to expand one's argument enough to acknowledge a diversity of opinion beyond the scope of the essay. Just as with writing a thesis, however, writing a sophisticated conclusion can be a challenging move from concrete understanding to abstract argument. In order to assist students in moving beyond repeating themselves at the end of essays, we offer the strategies in Figure 6.6. However, we give the caveat that sometimes, with beginning writers especially, we ask them not to conclude at all, to resist summing up, so that we can use their arguments as a springboard for future discussions and so we can resist teaching them a hollow structure that they must someday unlearn.

Figure 6.3

STRATEGY: DRAFTING A THESIS WHILE READING THE TEXT

First, use the following journal strategy from Chapter 4, Figure 4.2: Track a single character, symbol, or motif throughout a text. This works particularly well if students are also assigned a group with whom to track and discuss motif. (For example, in Kristi's class, this worked well with *The Awakening*—in the school year following the preceding story, of course—in which some students tracked the ocean, some clothing, some music, and so on.) Kimberly has also seen this approach work well with *The Great Gatsby*.

During each class session discussing the text, ask students to draft a clear sentence or two articulating what the motif (or character or symbol) seems to be doing and/or how it is changing in a text. Have students keep these sentences in their journals.

Write drafts of students' sentences on the board and have the class edit the sentences for clarity, omitting wordiness, ambiguous pronouns, and so on. This practice becomes an opportunity for solidifying skills taught in writing mini-lessons, for pushing students to put their personal responses into words, and for deepening arguments that are just grazing the surface (arguments about "happiness," for example).

At the end of the novel, students may already have a thesis to work with, drawn from one of their sentences. They will have at least gathered evidence and clarified their approach to motif (or character or symbol) so that writing an analytical essay on that specific literary feature becomes possible.

IDEAS FOR MODIFYING THIS STRATEGY

Assign a group essay or individual essay at the end of the unit that allows students to incorporate the drafting and group writing they have done throughout the unit.

Model tracking one specific motif, demonstrating the writing process every day, then have students practice this skill based on your model. In this way you can guide students through an understanding of where you found your ideas (specific quotations) and how you came to your conclusions.

Assign this strategy for a specific short story so that the text length is more manageable. Assign all students the same motif (or character or symbol), but have them write their clear sentence about one specific paragraph; this could work with an assigned paragraph or with a paragraph that students choose. (Kristi has experimented with this in her freshman English class, focusing on the role of the natural world in the short story "The Scarlet Ibis" by James Hurst.) Students can then write one paragraph using textual support, or a group or class essay using all of their ideas.

Assign several different poems or short texts and have students track the same image or idea in those different texts, readying for a discussion of how form helps writers explore ideas.

ASSESSMENT AND FEEDBACK

Conduct a discussion and collect feedback from the whole class when sentences are written on the board. In this way students receive feedback from the teacher and from other students and can see each other's ideas about the book.

Assign an analytical paragraph that students hand in for structured written feedback from the teacher. Such an assignment can support the development of their arguments and serve as a check for understanding.

Figure 6.4

STRATEGY: CRAFTING A THESIS AND DEFENDING IT VERBALLY
After students have reviewed quotations they have pulled from the book and information from each other's journals, ask them to write a draft thesis statement and organize all of their evidence. (This works best if they write or type all their evidence on one or two pages, but not necessarily in essay format.) Have students bring this thesis to a graded discussion in which they must defend their argument and challenge one another. We let students know how the discussion will be graded before they begin and ask them to help us establish ground rules for civilized discourse.
IDEAS FOR MODIFYING THIS STRATEGY Assign topics and ask students to gather evidence for discussion. Have students write a thesis statement as the final product *after* discussion has occurred. For beginning students, we provide model thesis statements and ask them to choose one to defend, then ask them to write a response discussing the difficulty or relative ease of defending an argument.
ASSESSMENT AND FEEDBACK Use a graded discussion as a crucial stage in the drafting process of a longer essay assignment. Grade this discussion as the final analytical product and do not require a full essay to be written after discussion takes place. Or assign an optional essay.

Figure 6.5

STRATEGY: USING CHILDREN'S BOOKS TO TEACH ARGUMENTATION AND THESIS WRITING
Select a children's book to use in class. We like *Click, Clack, Moo* by Doreen Cronin and *Naked Mole Rat Gets Dressed* by Mo Willems. These particular books have simple plot lines but surprising thematic complexity. It is easy for students to find something to discuss (word choice, characterization, setting, or dialogue, for example) and then to articulate how it connects to the author's purpose. Read the children's book aloud, asking students to keep notes on one specific aspect. For example, word choice, setting, characterization, dialogue, and so on. Have students use their notes to articulate a question about the text. It is often useful to review who, what, and why questions. Ask students to draft a thesis as the answer to the question.
IDEAS FOR MODIFYING THIS STRATEGY Allow students to work in pairs or small groups. Ask students to bring in their favorite children's book for this activity.
ASSESSMENT AND FEEDBACK Collect thesis drafts and respond to them. Ask students to help each other find support for proposed thesis statements and then craft a short outline of an essay that would prove their thesis.

Figure 6.6

STRATEGY: CONCLUSIONS AS REFLECTION ON THE WRITING PROCESS
After students have gathered evidence, crafted a thesis, and written a rough draft or outline, ask them to conclude the essay by answering one of the following questions. With a little practice (and some modeling from teachers and other student essays), students will begin to learn that restating the introduction will not answer these questions:
What did you learn about the subject in the course of writing this paper? What do you know now that you didn't know when you finished reading the text?
What is the significance of what you just argued? (We often call this "the big so what?")
IDEAS FOR MODIFYING THIS STRATEGY
Assign this strategy in class on the day a conclusion-free final paper is due. Model answering the questions for students and wander the room giving them feedback on the spot. In-class practice like this will help them feel more confident about writing a strong conclusion on their own for the next paper.
Fine-tune the word choice of the questions to suit your students, their writing level, and your unit plan.
Have students work with partners or very small groups to try to answer these questions for each other's papers.
ASSESSMENT AND FEEDBACK
For in-class writing, it is invaluable to have peers write reviews of their classmates' conclusions.
Assess the conclusion as part of an overall essay assignment.

In addition to the strategies in Figure 6.6, we have found it helpful for students to focus on conclusions in model essays, noting the ways conclusions can be structured and then trying at least two different conclusions for their own essays. We have also set up brief conferences specifically about conclusions. We ask students to summarize their argument verbally in the conference, then pose the question, "What is the significance of your argument?" Pushing students to answer in the moment may help them to realize the depth (or lack of depth) in their analysis.

USING MODEL ESSAYS TO ENHANCE THE DRAFTING PROCESS

As we acknowledged in Chapter 2, finding models of literary analysis that are appropriate for middle and high school level students can be difficult. We have found several online sources of strong student writing that can help. The Write Source online (www.thewritesource.com) offers student literary analysis and creative response, as does Norton's online guide to writing about literature (http://wwnorton.com/college/english/litweb10/writing/welcome.aspx). Our own models as well as student models remain our top choices. In spite of bemoaning "real-world" examples of literary analysis that suit the middle and high school classroom, we prefer to, again, focus on the thinking process inherent in articulating a claim and supporting it with confidence. Literature is our vehicle, essentially, for teaching students this crucial aspect of critical thinking.

We have had some success using published essays as models of specific skills we are trying to teach. Our running lists of skills we need to teach based on our students' previous writing inform our planning. The following section provides an example from Kristi's classroom on the impact of using George Orwell's writing to help unravel students' notion that an essay must follow a dull formula.

Teaching the Essays of George Orwell

Every year Kristi teaches several essays by George Orwell, and nothing helps students to write like reading an accomplished essayist. (All George Orwell essays are available in the public domain. For modeling introductions and thesis statements, Kristi recommends "A Hanging," "Marrakech," and "Revenge Is Sour.") Students usually respond to the essays using e-mail journals so that they have a conversation about the essays before they come to class (see journal and discussion strategies in Chapter 4). Although students have been asked to write essays, they have often spent very little time reading published essays. Kristi asks students to find Orwell's thesis in each essay they read, and they are often surprised that it is not at the end of the first paragraph. In fact, almost every Orwell essay they read begins with a lengthy introduction, filled with imagery, which introduces the speaker and his situation before it ever addresses his argument. The thesis is often worked in to the middle of a body paragraph after the situation has been introduced. This gives students insight into a way to involve the audience that ignores stock introductory phrases.

In addition to modeling introduction and thesis writing with Orwell's essays, Kristi has found Orwell's "Politics and the English Language" imperative to teaching students how to argue. A warning: this essay poses quite a challenge to students, and she recommends breaking it down into manageable parts, assigning specific segments and focused discussions on separate days. However, this essay has proven to be worth the work it requires. Kristi has students take each of Orwell's tenets for "bad writing" and create their own examples of bad writing. (See Appendix E3, "Orwell Group Writing," for the full activity directions.) Inevitably, every year she will have a student share an example of "bad writing" and then say, "This sounds like a thesis!" This opens the door for discussing what a thesis should do. Should it mystify the reader with complex vocabulary, or should it state its purpose in the clearest possible terms? What examples can students find from Orwell's writing? What examples can they find from their own essays? As homework, Kristi asks students to review any essays they still have on file and bring in their worst thesis. (If they do not have an old essay at home, she gives them a few topics on which to draft another example "bad" thesis at home.) Students then identify why the writing did not work and how they could fix it to argue more clearly. It works well to do this at the beginning of the year. It sets the tone for how Kristi wants students to approach argumentation and truly frees them from the notion that the more convoluted and obscure the thesis, the more educated they will sound. Students also gain an invaluable vocabulary for discussing their writing throughout the year.

To extend this lesson, Kristi has taught the Orwell essay and then assigned the reading of contemporary editorials in class, or examined language from contemporary political campaigns (her students had a field day with the words *hope*, *change*, and *maverick*, and candidates' corresponding arguments, during the 2008 presidential election), and contemporary satire (clips from *The Colbert Report* and *The Daily Show*, as well as print resources, work particularly well). Not only do students write better, but they will read their worlds with a more critical eye.

REVISION: STRUCTURE AND CRAFT

Once students have read models—professional, published models; teacher models; and student models—a conversation about structure and craft can happen readily. If students feel confident reading essays, we can start to ask them what they notice about the way a writer crafts his or her essays for impact. The preceding Orwell classroom example helps students at the higher levels, but what about our struggling readers and writers?

We work to remind ourselves that students will not master every step of analysis in the first essay, or in the first analytical paragraph that they write. For this reason we assign several analytical essays over the course of a semester, trimester, or year so that students can practice developing the critical reading and thinking skills that lead to strong writing. We have had success starting middle school students as well as freshmen with analytical paragraphs, followed by writing a short essay. Including two or three revision lessons in one unit plan is sufficient, especially if these lessons are created in response to past essays. For example, we keep track of frequent student errors in essays from one unit and then craft lessons in response to those errors for the next unit. Most mini-lessons on revision come after students have begun writing so that they are free to first think about the text and their argument, *then* polish their language and ideas. We have included several sample lessons in Appendix E. They address the following errors specific to analytical writing, which we find and combat in student writing every year:

- Quotation formatting (Appendix E1, "Incorporating Quotation Practice")
- Avoiding wordiness (Appendix E4, "Word Economy")
- Practicing use of strong verbs (Appendix E5, "The Beauty of Strong Verbs")

In-Class Conferencing

We have learned that if we want students to engage in the messy process of drafting and revising in support of structure and craft, we need to provide time and coaching in class. We cannot wait until they turn in their work to point out what they need to fix. And in some cases, we need to work with students to get them started on writing and keep them going.

Sometimes at the end of a class writing session, we ask students to submit their rough drafts with a marked section and a sticky note telling what they want feedback on. We then read through these drafts and respond with a note addressing their question or concern.

More typically, we use students' drafts as the basis for mini-conferences. We return the drafts the day after we collect them and let students know we will get to them for a mini-conference but that they can work on other sections while we make our way around the room. Because we have skimmed through the drafts, we have determined which students need help first.

We recognize that when we have multiple classes drafting essays, this kind of overnight skimming is not practical. So we use the same idea, but during class writing time. We ask students to mark a section of their draft and frame a question they want to discuss so that when we do have a mini-conference, they are ready. It is helpful to model asking a question about a draft essay we are writing ourselves. This targeted approach to conferencing helps us avoid the situation in which a student wants us to listen to his or her entire draft or has a number of questions or has not yet started writing and wants us to do their writing with (for) them.

Typically during mini-conferences we ask students to "say more" in the section they have marked by adding a quote or more detail in explanation of the quote they have included. Or we may ask a question that focuses students' attention on the way they have written the essay section or points them back to the text. We have also found it helpful to make notes during the conference as the student shares thoughts and then give these notes to the student. In some cases, we invite the student to dictate their revisions to us; this keeps their focus on the thinking and we can ask clarifying questions as we write down their words. One freshman student was shocked when Kimberly handed him the draft he had dictated to her. "Wow," he said, "I said some great stuff."

Mini-conferences, and the draft skimming we described, provide us with mini-lesson topics. If we observe a pattern in a number of students' essays that needs to be addressed, we will teach a mini-lesson to the whole class. We have found it helpful to ask students to apply the mini-lesson to their draft and mark these sections in their draft. We can then circulate and check their application. We also have found it effective to have students write an exit note in which they provide an example of how they applied the mini-lesson. We can then skim through the exit notes and follow up with students if needed.

We feel compelled to admit that we struggle with in-class conferencing. We value the one-on-one teaching it allows, but find it very challenging to provide each student with the conference time they need. We have tried conferencing with small groups of students, with limited success. So in addition to conferencing with students, we create opportunities for students to conference with each other, but with clear guidelines.

Focused Peer Response

We recommend using peer response at multiple stages in the writing process. As we have mentioned throughout the book, modeling is essential. For modeling peer response we use a sample essay or section of an essay—usually one we have written—and provide students with a specific feedback focus. They respond to our sample as a whole class before they take on the role of responding to a peer.

We have had students respond to their peers' introduction paragraphs and thesis statements in peer response groups by responding to this question: What is the writer promising to prove (their thesis)? But we have also had great success using Linda Christensen's (2009) "Thesis Statement Wall," where students post their thesis statements on strips of paper, without their names, around the room. Students then circulate and read through statements. A discussion follows, with an emphasis on what makes a good thesis. We concur with Christensen's suggestion to highlight examples of strong thesis statements, and to follow up individually with students whose thesis statements may need some further work or development. This conversation about thesis statements helps students understand the role of the thesis and articulate their thinking in support of their thesis.

Over the years we have found it helpful to have students provide written feedback to each other as well as verbal. We provide a peer response form for their written feedback (see Appendix E6, "Peer Review Guidelines"). It is our preference to have student writers read aloud to their peer response group the draft of the section they are focusing on, but we ask group members to silently fill out the feedback form before sharing their comments with the whole group. We have found that three or four students in a group works best. It can also be effective to have students work as pairs, which allows for more detailed feedback.

Sometimes we have peers read through "almost final" drafts of essays with a checklist to use for feedback. The checklist usually contains specific information that we have taught according to our unit plan: apostrophes, for example, or quotation integration. This process can be done in pairs so that students can talk about the feedback. But we have also found it effective to assign drafts to peers to read and then collect the feedback sheets and return them to the student author. This allows us to pick which student serves as the peer responder for each draft. And for some groups of students, we read through the peer responses before we return them to the student authors. We have even found it effective to conference with peer responders about their response, helping them to be more specific or to clarify their comments. We have learned that using a peer response form or protocol is critical to this process (in addition to the form in Appendix E6, see Christensen 2009, page 146, and Elbow and Belanoff 2000, which contains multiple peer response protocols).

FOSTERING THINKING BEYOND FORMULA

Ultimately, we need to remind the students (and ourselves) to be patient with the process of writing an analytical essay. "An imposed structure, even when it does not fit the content well, can make writing look stronger than it really is, at least at first glance" (Spandel 2005, 121). So when we remove common formulas and structure class time and instruction to foster student ideas, we will no doubt end up with "messy" writing, especially as we begin teaching in this way.

With younger writers, it is important to value content over form right away so that they learn that analytical writing requires time, effort, extensive revision, and thought. With older writers, be ready for what Kristi calls "the pendulum shift" essays: the first essay that removes specific structure requirements and instead allows freedom can come as a shock, especially to students who have been rewarded for years for bland essays. Inevitably, that first essay shows a student hard at work, but disorganized in his or her approach. As one student told Kristi when writing a poetry essay, "I have never felt more confident about my thoughts on an essay and have never worked harder. But the structure is all over the place." On the first essay of the year, this is a good position for the student. For her, the pendulum has swung to the disorganized but thoughtful side of the continuum. On the next essay, it will probably swing in the opposite direction: still thoughtful, but with each sentence painstakingly structured. By the end of the year, her final essay will fall right in the middle. As teachers, we must be patient with this process and allow students to experience the frustration that comes with real learning, and what Vygotsky (1962, 1978) calls "disequilibrium." We need to communicate clearly what we value: not rote responses to a text, but a student *learning* to push his or her brain past concrete initial impressions. As Vicki Spandel reminds us in her book *The 9 Rights of Every Writer*:

> Being yourself. Telling the truth. Taking a closer look. Those are the things a writer cannot survive without. Technique is just frosting on the cake. We make a mistake when we begin with technique. We need to begin with our students, who they are, what they feel. Writing lives inside of us. (2005, 125)

CHAPTER 7

WRITING WITH MENTORS

Throughout this book we have touted the importance of reading a variety of literature: novels, short stories, plays, essays, memoirs, children's books, and graphic novels. This variety reflects the range of choices authors have in sharing their stories, experiences, ideas, and emotions with readers. We want students to have this range of choices in writing about literature:

> As English teachers our major responsibility is to enfranchise students in our classes to such a degree that they think of themselves as writers, as those who use written language to both discover thinking and communicate thought, who boldly try varied forms of writing, using them to meet their needs. (Romano, 1987, 131)

These responses to literature can take place anywhere in a unit. As noted in Chapter 2, we use our unit objectives to identify what we want students to know, understand, and be able to do. We then use these objectives to determine the assessments we will ask of students. We have used the writing responses described in this chapter as final or summative assessments. We have also used them as preassessments to gather information about students' understanding of a genre or writing craft before we immerse them in more reading in that genre or focusing on that craft. And we have found that these responses work well as ongoing assessments in the midst of teaching a unit.

We want to share our learning about the importance of clear criteria regarding assessment. Both of us have experienced students completing a literature-inspired response, only to discover the student did not have a good working knowledge of the text. We learned to include assessment criteria that require links to the text.

This chapter is divided into two sections, "Literature as Mentor," which focuses on responses that rely on both the content and structure of the mentor text, and "Literature as Inspiration," which focuses on responses that draw on the content of a text to create a response in a different genre. We recognize that there is crossover between these two sections. And we are compelled to admit that our enthusiasm for these responses has resulted in a number of examples with short descriptions. It is a "more is more" approach in terms of quantity and a "less is more" approach in terms of detail. When we shared drafts of this chapter with colleagues, we were pleased to see that the responses we listed led to lively discussions of how they have used these ideas as well as ways they want to try new ideas in their classrooms. It also led to great stories about other kinds of responses. Inspired, we got permission from colleagues to add their ideas to the chapter. We hope you'll have a similar reaction: you will be affirmed in the responses you are already using and discover new ideas and strategies.

LITERATURE AS MENTOR

In this section we explore writing in the form of the literature that students are reading and analyzing: a poem to reflect on a poem, a character sketch based on the reading of a short story with rich character development, an essay that draws on the structure of essays students have studied. This takes the concept that we read literature as a model for good writing and makes the modeling explicit. Students are asked to step into the structure and voice of an author's work—to try it on. Tom Romano writes,

> **Imitation of an author's ways with words can create a gush of language. Imitation can cut loose a voice and let writers experience the power that comes with a little recklessness, a little letting go of the self and learning the language rhythms and voice habits of another. (2004, 101)**

Essays

We are inspired by the wealth of essays available to use with students. We have included some of our favorite, student-tested essay explorations in this chapter, as well as in the Suggested Works list at the end of the book.

One of our favorite essay resources is the This I Believe Web site (http://thisibelieve.org), which has over 90,000 essays arranged by theme, such as courage, creativity, social justice, education and knowledge, and even pets and animals. A number of the essays also include a podcast so that students can hear the author read his or her own work as they follow along. We have had students read an essay first and then reread it as they listened to the author read it aloud. Students frequently comment on how the essay takes on new meaning when they hear it read by its author. As one student noted, "It's like the words come to life."

This I Believe essays can be used to explore structure and craft by asking students to note the use of an explicit or implied thesis, or the use of personal examples, or how the essay incorporates quotes from other sources. Students then write their own This I Believe essay using the craft and structures of one or several of the essays.

We have also used This I Believe essays in support of a study of theme. Students read and listen to a selection of essays on a particular theme, such as creativity, tolerance, courage, or social justice. They then write their own This I Believe essay on a theme of their choice.

The This I Believe Web site provides resources for educators as well as a place for students to publish their work.

We have listed in Figure 7.1 some of our favorite essays from the Web site and how we have used them to illustrate essay craft and structure as well as theme. We have included essays written by teens at the end of the list, not because they are less important but so that they are clustered together if you want to use only essays written by young authors.

Figure 7.1
OUR FAVORITE THIS I BELIEVE ESSAYS

ESSAY TITLE	AUTHOR	ESSAY STRUCTURE/THEME
"In Giving I Connect With Others" http://thisibelieve.org/essay/11	Isabel Allende (author of novels and essays)	Essay Structure: thesis, examples Theme: death, family, goodness and kindness
"The Joy and Enthusiasm of Reading" http://thisibelieve.org/essay/31	Rick Moody (author of *The Ice Storm* and short stories)	Essay Structure: references to literature, parallelism Theme: creativity, education and knowledge, why we read
"Do What You Love" http://thisibelieve.org/essay/22870	Tony Hawk (professional skateboarder)	Essay Structure: thesis, contrast Theme: creativity, family, work
"Creative Solutions to Life's Challenges" http://thisibelieve.org/essay/21253	Frank X. Walker (poet)	Essay Structure: thesis, repetition Theme: creativity, family, purpose
"An Invitation to Dialogue" http://thisibelieve.org/essay/14142	Madhukar Rao	Essay Structure: reflection on personal vignette Themes: race, tolerance
"Inner Strength from Desperate Times" http://thisibelieve.org/26941	Jake Hovendar (high school student)	Essay Structure: personal vignette Themes: courage, family, gratitude

Figure 7.1 (continued)

"Returning to What's Natural" http://thisibelieve.org/essay/13023	Amelia Baxter-Stolzfus (high school student)	Essay Structure: variation on thesis, examples, voice Theme: change
"Being Content With Myself" http://thisibelieve.org/essay/10490	Kamaal Majeed (high school student)	Essay Structure: question lead, personal vignette Theme: prejudice, race, tolerance, self-determination
"We're All Different in Our Own Ways" http://thisibelieve.org/essay/14338	Joshua Yuchasz (high school student)	Essay Structure: question lead, examples Theme: equality, tolerance
"Tomorrow Will Be a Better Day" http://thisibelieve.org/essay/4205	Josh Rittenberg (high school student)	Essay Structure: personal vignette, examples Themes: family, hope

This I Believe essays illustrate the power of the "personal vignette." As noted in Chapter 5, personal vignette/text-to-self connections can be an effective component of essays about literature. And, although not the topic of this book, we have found that developing personal vignettes can support students in writing essays for college applications. For more on this, we recommend "Writing the College Essay: Creating a Vision of Possibility," a chapter in Linda Christensen's book *Reading, Writing, and Rising Up* (2000).

We encourage students to take the inspiration they get from reading This I Believe essays to effect change by writing a business letter to a person or organization who could make change happen (see the "Literature as Inspiration" section of this chapter for a discussion of this response).

Kristi's husband, Dylan Hardy, used published essays to help his students write about the ways in which their lives connected to the larger world. His independent-study students used George Orwell's essays "Shooting an Elephant," "A Hanging," "Revenge Is Sour," and "Marrakech" as mentor texts. After discussing how Orwell often begins his essays with a vivid personal anecdote and eventually makes a political point, students read a modern essay from *Wired* magazine, "One Million Workers. 90 Million iPhones. 17 Suicides. Who's to Blame?" In it, writer Joel Johnson wonders if, because he enjoys his affordable and convenient iPhone, he is somehow responsible for the deaths of workers at an iPhone manufacturing plant in China. Students then wrote essays in which they identified an individual concern in their own lives and connected it to a larger political issue. For example, one student began an essay with the image of dropping her possessions in a crowded high school hallway and struggling to pick them up in time for class. She explored the idea that, had she been near only one or two people, they would have helped, but the masses moving through the halls ignored her plight. She concluded that in such a crowded world, it is easy for a group to ignore an individual's needs.

Memoirs

Another use of the personal vignette is in memoir. In the essay, the personal vignette is used as an example in support of the essay's theme or argument. In a memoir, the personal vignette is detailed to illustrate a life lesson. We recognize that this distinction can be subtle. But for purposes of this section, we explore students using memoirs, or more likely, excerpts from memoirs, to examine craft and structure in support of writing their own memoir. As William Zinsser notes, "A good memoir requires two elements—one of art and the other of craft" (1998, 6).

As an introduction to the art and craft of this genre, we embrace the "six-word" memoir. According to the editors of *What I Was Planning: Six Word Memoirs by Writers Famous and Obscure* (Fershleiser and Smith 2008), the legend is that Hemingway was challenged to write a story in six words, and he created "For sale: baby shoes, never worn." Whether the legend is true or not, the six-word story was born. The online magazine SMITH sponsored a contest in 2006 inviting authors to write six-word memoirs, which were then published in a collection (Fershleiser and Smith 2008). These are among the results:

> "Semicolons; I use them to excess." by Iris Page
> "Nobody cared, then they did. Why?" by Chuck Klosterman
> "Wounded girl turns life into stories." by Farai Chideya
> "Me see world! Me write stories." by Elizabeth Gilbert
> "My second grade teacher was right." by Janelle Brown
> "Never liked the taste of beets." by Michael Pemberton

You can also find six-word memoir inspiration on this companion Web site to SMITH magazine: http://www.sixwordmemoir.com.

We have witnessed inspired six-word memoirs authored by sixth graders and high school juniors and seniors. Mollie Dickson's sixth-grade students embraced the six-word memoir:

"Fight like a girl. You'll win." by Marissa
"Lots to hide. Less to tell." by Taelor
"Walk, don't run, through your life." by Connor
"Spontaneous: The jump I cannot make." by Kiley

After reading six-word memoirs, juniors and seniors in a creative writing class taught by Kara Wendel were inspired to write their own:

"Treading through waters of the past." by Bradie
"I'm fat but I am tender." by Shanji
"Internal assessment due Tomorrow: bad words." by Vivian
I'm worried, thinking, twisted, and . . . shrinking." by Chelsea

And in recognition of how six words can lead to longer memoirs, Sam wrote, "I need more than six words."

Figure 7.2
OUR FAVORITE MEMOIR MENTORS

TITLE	AUTHOR	TOPIC/FOCUS	LITERARY CRAFT
"In the Blink of an Eye"	Norma Fox Mazer	Childhood	Grabber lead Descriptive details
"Being Mean"	Gary Soto	Childhood	Grabber lead
"Extreme Clean Sports"	Laurie Notaro	Family	Character details
Excerpt from *Black Boy*, pages 91–93	Richard Wright	Family confrontation	Dialogue
"The Long Closet"	Jane Yolen	Childhood	Descriptive details of grandparents' closet
Excerpt from *An American Childhood*, pages 20–23	Annie Dillard	Childhood	Descriptive details of Pittsburgh, PA
Excerpt from *A Girl Named Zippy*, pages 120–124	Haven Kimmel	Family	Dialogue

Memoir excerpts work well as mentors for students writing longer memoirs. We appreciate the collection *When I Was Your Age, Volume Two* edited by Amy Erlich, because it contains memoirs of childhood written by YA authors. Students can see how authors they have read tell the story of their own childhood: they focus on details of a particular moment or event to illustrate that although each of us is unique, we can find solace and inspiration in each other's stories of childhood.

We appreciate memoirs that focus on lessons from childhood and family, topics that our students can easily connect to their own lives. And we are grateful for the ways memoirs illustrate writing craft. We have listed in Figure 7.2 a selection of memoirs that work well as mentors for students, and we note the topic/focus as well as literary craft involved.

It's been our experience that good memoir examples inspire students to write good memoirs. We have found it helpful to have students complete a self-reflection after writing their memoir, in which they comment on how they used the sample memoirs in support of their writing. At the conclusion of her unit on memoir, which included reading a variety of memoir excerpts, teacher Carrie Strecker asked her tenth-grade students to respond to the following self-evaluation questions:

1. *What inspired your memoir piece? Please name any readings or writing prompts that helped.*
2. *I told you I would be grading you partially on what you took from the memoir reading and how you used it to make your writing more effective. With this in mind, what should I look for while reading your piece?*

Eulogies

Adlai Stevenson wrote a moving tribute to Eleanor Roosevelt. Kimberly used this eulogy as part of a modern nonfiction unit in a junior English class. Students heard the eulogy read aloud as they followed along in the text. They then reread it and highlighted the excerpt, using one color for examples of virtues and another color for accomplishments. A third reading focused on Stevenson's use of contrasts:

> **A woman whose lucid and luminous faith testified always for sanity in an insane time and for hope in a time of obscure hope—a woman who spoke for the good toward which man aspires in a world which has seen too much of the evil of which man is capable. (Stevenson 1997, 102)**

Kimberly shared her own eulogy for her beloved aunt Martha. In it she remembered with fondness how her aunt taught her to bake, her aunt's willingness to listen and ask good questions, and her throaty laugh, which was a compelling illustration of her ability to find humor even in difficult times.

Students' own eulogies of beloved relatives, cats, dogs, hamsters, and even a surprisingly moving eulogy of Bessie Lou, who is revealed to be a stolen Honda Civic at the very end of the eulogy, illustrated students' understanding of the genre and, in many cases, the use of contrasts, as modeled by Adlai Stevenson. Students commented on their appreciation for learning how to write a eulogy—knowing this would be a real writing task in their futures. The surprise was the interest they showed in Eleanor Roosevelt. Stevenson's eulogy allowed them to know her as a person, not as just a historical figure.

Figure 7.3 details a strategy that supports students writing a eulogy.

Figure 7.3

STRATEGY: EULOGY AS MENTOR
Hand out photocopies of a eulogy.
Ask students to read it and mark/highlight details they gather about the person/pet being eulogized.
Follow with a second reading in which students note the structure of the eulogy.
Have students create a list of people, pets, or even lost "treasures" that they want to honor with a eulogy.
Model your own eulogy.
From a selection of eulogies, have students choose one to three examples and read them, noting details and structure that they can use in support of their writing.
Have students draft their own eulogy.
In peer revision groups, have students share their eulogies, returning to the sample eulogies in support of their revision efforts.
Ask students to share their eulogies aloud with the class.
IDEAS FOR MODIFYING THIS STRATEGY
Have students use the format of a selected eulogy in support of writing their own.
Have students work in pairs to craft a eulogy of a classroom object.
ASSESSMENT AND FEEDBACK
Ask students to provide written feedback on their peers' eulogies.
Ask students to self-evaluate their eulogy, noting how it reflects what they learned from reading eulogies.
Give students feedback on their presentation and their written eulogy.

We recognize that eulogies can take on different forms: tributes, editorials, and essays. But at the heart of this writing is the opportunity to acknowledge and celebrate the life of another. As Phyllis Theroux, editor of *The Book of Eulogies*, writes, "It is in the questions, judgments, and attempts to understand a completed life that a eulogy can speak to us" (1997, 16).

Figure 7.4
OUR FAVORITE EULOGY MODELS

SUBJECT OF EULOGY	AUTHOR OF EULOGY
Emily Dickinson	An editorial tribute written by her sister-in-law, Susan Gilbert Dickinson (1997)
Walt Whitman	Eulogy by politician Robert Ingersoll (1997)
Henry David Thoreau	Eulogy by Ralph Waldo Emerson (1997)
Mark Twain	Eulogy by Rev. Henry Van Dyke, longtime friend (2003)
Virginia Woolf	Tribute by Christopher Isherwood, literary colleague and friend (2003)
Helen Keller	Eulogy by Sen. Lister Hill, Alabama (2003)
William Stafford	Tribute by his son and fellow poet, Kim Stafford (1997)
Theodor Seuss Geisel	Eulogy by Robert Bernstein, publisher and friend (2003)
John Fitzgerald Kennedy	Tribute to Kennedy and his visit to Ireland by Sean Quinlan, Irish poet (1997)
Martin Luther King Jr.	Eulogy by Benjamin May, president of Morehouse College, longtime friend and mentor (2003)
Lucille Ball	Eulogy by Diane Sawyer (2003)
Charles Schulz	Eulogy by Cathy Guisewite, friend and creator of comic strip *Cathy* (2003)
George Harrison	Eulogy by Eric Idle (2003)
Arthur Ashe	*New York Times* (1997)
John Conrad Jr.	Eulogy by his father, John Conrad Sr. (1997)
John F. Kennedy Jr.	Eulogy by Sen. Edward Kennedy (2003)
Kevin Smith's "Pop"	A moving tribute to his father by Kevin Smith, author, film director, and actor (2007)
Daisy	A humorous yet moving eulogy of his beloved dog by E. B. White (1997)
"Mr. Smith Goes to Heaven"	Essay tribute to her beloved dog by Anna Quindlen (1993)

It has been our experience that eulogies and other forms of memorial tribute both move and inspire students. We have listed here some additional examples that support students' in writing their own tributes. And please see our exploration of eulogies with fictional characters in the "Literature as Inspiration" section of this chapter.

We note that the examples listed in Figure 7.4 can be used to meet curriculum requirements regarding reading and writing nonfiction.

Poetry Copy-Change

Poetry lends itself to close reading and rereading. We have witnessed the discoveries students make when they "try on" the language and structure of a mentor poem by writing their own poem using the mentor poem as a model. Students can speak to the craft of the poem using the language of poetry: metaphor, simile, personification, rhyme, rhythm, line breaks, stanza. Stephen Dunning and William Stafford refer to this technique of beginning with a published poem and writing a new poem using the original poem to guide and inspire their efforts as "copy-change" (1992, 90).

William Carlos Williams's poems work well for this, in particular "The Red Wheelbarrow" and "This Is Just to Say" (1991). We have also enjoyed watching students copy-change Emily Dickinson's poem "This Is My Letter to the World" and the first section of Walt Whitman's "Song of Myself." (See Kimberly Campbell's *Less Is More: Teaching Literature with Short Texts, Grades 6–12*, pages 165–169, for more on teaching these poets and copy-change.) Kristi's students, both freshmen and seniors, have created masterful poems about something they know well and love to observe based on Wallace Stevens's "Thirteen Ways of Looking at a Blackbird."

Shakespeare's sonnets also work well for copy-change. We have provided students with a copy of a sonnet with words removed and invited them to fill in their word choices. This also helps in the understanding of poetry craft: iambic pentameter, tone, and voice. We have also asked students to pick from a selection of sonnets and rewrite one using some of Shakespeare's words and lines as well as weaving in their own. We have often followed this activity with a study of Billy Collins's poem "Sonnet" (2001) and invited students to use it as another mentor poem for copy-change.

The wonderful book *A Note Slipped Under the Door* uses a mentor poem at the beginning of each chapter to explore aspects of poetry craft. The authors, Nick Flynn and Shirley McPhillips, explain that in selecting mentor poems, "the first criterion . . . is that it be a poem we love, that moves us in some way, intellectually, emotionally, or spiritually" (2000, 3). They go on to remind us of poet Robert Pinsky's words, "Art is best understood through careful attention to great examples" (Pinsky quoted in Flynn and McPhillips 2000, 4).

An unexpected but delightful result of copy-change is that students develop a relationship with the poets they rely on as mentors. They come to know the poem and poet in a new way. Teacher Erin Ocon noticed that when the middle school students with whom she works spent time with William Stafford's poetry as mentors, they began to talk about him as a fellow writer. They would note places where they used his style and would also note things like, "So in this stanza, I went a different direction than William by adding an extra line." When Kimberly worked with juniors to copy-change a section of Walt Whitman's "Song of Myself," she noticed students were talking about free verse, rhythm, tone, parallel structure, and Walt. They were on a first-name basis with the poet with whom they explored poetry craft. (See further discussion of Walt in the "Character Conversations Across Texts and/or Time" section of this chapter.)

Poem Parodies and Copy-Change

Kristi discovered that students who are not fans of a particular poet can make discoveries about his or her craft by writing in the voice of the poet. After exploring Robert Frost and Sylvia Plath, with mixed reviews on the part of students, she invited them to use copy-change to write a parody of the work of one of the poets. Kristi modeled her own example, "IB English Song," based on Sylvia Plath's "Morning Song." It reflects her feelings from her first year of teaching. She explained this to students, read the poem with them, and set them in motion with the following instructions:

For three weeks we have labored through Frost and Plath, sharing moments of darkness, moments of light. It is time for the poem analyzers to become the poets.

Over the weekend, I'd like you to play with language. Your mission is to write a parody of either Frost or Plath, or what I call a copy-change poem. Try your hand at all of the literary devices we have talked about. Think about where you can use assonance, consonance, alliteration, precise diction, rhyme, and rhythm. How will you structure your poem? How will you create tone?

The objective is to get you playing with poetry and internalizing some of the knowledge you have of literary devices. You may write about any subject you choose, but try on Frost's and Plath's patterns for size (i.e., write and reflect their approach to poetry).

Your poems are due in class on Tuesday. Be prepared to share your work with small groups and/or the whole class if you feel brave. You will display (publish!) the poems on the back wall of the class.

Poems should be a minimum of eight lines long, but there is no maximum length. Strive for originality. Humor is welcome.

Go forth and explore your desert places!

Among the most memorable student poems from the first year Kristi used this assignment were one student's "Dessert Places," modeled after Robert Frost's "Desert Places," and "The Laundry Woman's Complaint," modeled after Plath's "The Queen's Complaint" (see Figure 7.5). The students took pride in their poetry and truly adopted their chosen poet's style. In the process, they developed a recognition of and, for some, an appreciation of the poet's craft.

Pastiche

Pastiche builds on the idea of copy-change in poetry by inviting students to understand a text by adopting the style of the text. "A pastiche is an exercise in literary criticism: it involves changing one or more elements of a work in prose or poetry in order to examine the effects of stylistic variation" (Webb 2006, 1). The student uses the original text as the model, taking on the style of the author while creating a new text. In the process students develop an understanding of the craft of the text. The goal is "likeness." "A pastiche is very like that which it pastiches. In some cases, it may be all but indistinguishable from it, in others more obviously different, but it must always seem pretty close" (Dyer 2007, 54).

The play *Rosencrantz and Guildenstern Are Dead* by Tom Stoppard is an example of a pastiche of *Hamlet*. Stories featuring the character of Sherlock Holmes are examples of pastiche based on the character created by Sir Arthur Conan Doyle.

The International Baccalaureate curriculum includes pastiche as a creative response to literature, defining it as

> **an imitation or re-creation of an already published work. In this assignment, the candidate is encouraged to demonstrate his/her sensitivity to, and understanding of, a work by providing an original composition after the manner of the text. The candidate must include, within the prescribed word limit, an evaluation of his/her aims and achievement. (International Baccalaureate Requirements 2002)**

A colleague of Kristi's, Lori Townzen, uses this response option with IB juniors for *Their Eyes Were Watching God* (see her instructions to students in Appendix F1).

Figure 7.5
STUDENT'S POEM USING PLATH'S POEM AS MENTOR

THE QUEEN'S COMPLAINT by Sylvia Plath	THE LAUNDRY WOMAN'S COMPLAINT by Caitlin Marineau *Dedicated to my broken dryer*
In ruck and quibble of courtfolk This giant hulked, I tell you, on her scene With hands like derricks, Looks fierce and black as rooks; Why, all the windows broke when he stalked in.	In ruck and piles of mud-caked laundry This machine tumbled, I tell you, in her house With lint catchers like fly traps, Dials clicking and spinning as clocks; Why, all the racks broke when he plugged in.
Her dainty acres he ramped through And used her gentle doves with manners rude; I do not know What fury urged him slay Her antelope who meant him naught but good.	Her dainty thongs he ramped through And used her gentle lingerie with manners rude; I do not know What heat setting made him shrink Her flower-speckled pjs who meant naught but to be dried.
She spoke most chiding in his ear Till he some pity took upon her crying; Of rich attire He made her shoulders bare And solaced her, but quit her at cock's crowing.	She beat most furiously on his top Till he took some pity on her drying; Of sweat shirts and pants He made her body bare And took her clothes, but crippled at her bid of starting.

A hundred heralds she sent out
To summon in her slight all doughty men
Whose force might fit
Shape of her sleep, her thought—
None of that greenhorn lot matched her bright
    crown.
	A hundred phone calls she sent out
	To summon to her sight all appliance repair men
	Whose parts might fit
	Shape of the tubes, the dials—
	None of that cigarette-smoking, crack-baring lot could dry
	    her dripping socks.

So she is come to this rare pass
Whereby she treks in blood through sun and
    squall
And sings you thus:
"How sad, alas, it is
To see my people shrunk so small, so small."
	So she is come to this dust-bunnied pass
	Behind the machine she treks in lost underwear through
	    dirt and lint
	And grits her teeth annoyed:
	"How sad, alas, it is
	To see my pants shrunk so small, so small."

We have seen pastiche used with *The House on Mango Street* by Sandra Cisneros. Students take chapters in the book and imitate Cisneros's style to write their own stories based on her chapter topics: "Hairs," "My Name," or student-selected chapters that explore neighbors and the neighborhood. We have also used *The House on Mango Street* as the inspiration for rewriting a newspaper article in Cisneros's style. In the process students explore the use of figurative language and run-on sentences to tell a story. Kristi recommends the use of Cisnero's table of contents as a model for students to title the events in their own lives. (See a lesson plan by Erin Carlson [2011] for using the table of contents at http://urbandreams.ousd.k12.ca.us/lessonplans/mango_street2/index.htm.)

Eudora Welty's short story "A Worn Path" is a compelling sketch of character Phoenix Jackson. We come to know her through the vivid description of her journey to get medicine for her grandson. Students in Kimberly's junior English class used Welty's story as a mentor for writing their own character sketch. Their task was to create a brief scene in which we come to know the character through their clothing, the way they walk, their speech, and their interactions with others.

Kimberly was surprised to find a framed character sketch one of her students wrote about her, with Eudora Welty as his mentor. Sadly the student was leaving school, but he left a note explaining that he valued this writing and wanted her to have it. The framed original sits in a place of honor on the bookshelf in Kimberly's office.

We have also used David Sedaris's hilarious pastiche of what happens when his encounter with a Shakespearean actor inspires him to speak in Shakespearean language in response to everyday life events. This story was aired on the radio program *This American Life* and can be found at this Web site: http://www.npr.org/templates/story/story.php?storyid=1109147. Or read the chapter "The Drama Bug" in Sedaris's collection of essays *Naked* (1997).

We have delighted in students' Shakespearean language pastiches, which have included conversations with car mechanics, discussions with parents regarding curfew, a misunderstanding with a friend (including a sword fight), and a romantic scene staged on a deck rather than a balcony. A structured conversation in Shakespeare's style can also be an excellent introduction to his language. Kristi's colleague Joe Dessert models a basic conversation and elements of Shakespeare's language to help students understand the text using the format from *Shakespeare Set Free* (O'Brien 1993, 54–55).

We also have used pastiche to explore changing an element of a literary text. The goal is to rewrite a portion of the text, trying on the author's voice. As Tom Romano notes, "Imitating the forms of professionals is fun, instructive, and confidence-building.

The model usually provides just the right amount of framework to lead students into their own language" (1987, 136). In the examples that follow we explore this use of pastiche: changing an element of a literary text.

Write a New Ending

Students in Rachel Pass's alternative high school English class were disappointed by the ending to the novel *Paranoid Park* by Blake Nelson; they asked for the option of writing a new ending as their summative assignment. They had become invested in the characters and wanted more closure than the author's ending provided. Most students chose to write in the third-person narrator from the original text and create one new chapter ending. But one student wrote several chapters for her new ending; each chapter represented a different character's point of view. This new ending option was one of several in response to this book. Rachel shared with us that she had asked students to track a theme throughout their reading of the text in support of the creative response they would be required to complete (see Chapter 3 for more on close reading of theme), and she provided the scoring rubric for the final assessment before students began to read. She was pleased to see students refer to this rubric in pitching the addition of "write a new ending" to the list of final project choices. For each of the options, a requirement was that students include quotes from the text with their analysis. But they had options for the form of their completed project.

This approach also works well with short stories. Students in an eighth-grade English class wrote a new ending to Cynthia Rylant's "Checkouts." The story ends with the two characters going their separate ways. Asking the question, "What would happen if the characters got together?" allowed students to revisit details in the story and use them in support of their new ending. Many students chose to write happy endings.

Change the Setting

Students can move a scene to a new location or to a new time period. Students in a senior English class explored how the character Beowulf would be treated if he came to the present day. They were particularly intrigued by how he would deal with women. And what if *The Catcher in the Rye* by J. D. Salinger was set in their high school? How would they deal with Holden Caufield?

Rewrite the Text from a Different Point of View

For this option, students choose or are provided with a text excerpt that involves more than one character. They are asked to rewrite the excerpt from a different point of view.

In Laurie Halse Anderson's novel *Speak*, the narrator, Melinda, is forced to meet with her school counselor and parents. How would Melinda's parents tell the story of meeting with the school counselor? What might the school counselor say?

Teacher Rachel Pass asked students to respond to a key scene in the short story "Bullet in the Brain" by Tobias Wolff. In the original text, the narrator, Anders, a book critic, is a customer at a bank. He converses with a woman who is waiting in front of him in the line for a teller. Suddenly bank robbers enter the bank; Anders has an encounter with one of the robbers and is shot. Anders relives memories from his life as the bullet passes through his brain. What would the bank robber with the gun say about this scene? What about the companion bank robber? The bank teller? Or guard? And the woman Anders spoke to in line—what would she tell us?

Conversations Between Characters
This response can be used as a low-stakes journal entry in support of students' reading of a text. It can also be used in support of a literature circle discussion; students can volunteer or be assigned different character pairs and craft a conversation they then share during a literature circle discussion. We have also used this response effectively as a final assessment of a text. The prompts include asking students to craft conversations that could take place during the course of the text. We have also created prompts that build on the text by asking students to draw on what they know about the character and how he or she would respond in a new setting. Here are sample prompts:

- What might Gene and Finny say to each other if Finny did not die in *A Separate Peace*? Consider the conversation that might take place at their twenty-year high school reunion.
- What would Scout and her father talk about over dinner a year after the trial in *To Kill a Mockingbird*? Ten years after the trial?
- If Gatsby did not die, what might Nick and he discuss if they ran into each other?
- What might the fathers of Romeo and Juliet say to each other at the end of the play?
- What would Odysseus (from *The Odyssey*) say to Poseidon?
- If the character of Lily, from *The Secret Life of Bees* by Sue Monk Kidd, could bring her mother back for one day, what would they discuss? And if she had a conversation with her father at the end of the book, what might they say?

Transform a Character or Characters

This response idea was inspired by a student who asked, "I wonder how the story would be different if Huckleberry Finn was a girl?" A lively discussion followed. We have since used this inspiration during the reading and as a final response to a text. We have provided students with specific chapters or scenes as options to use for this response. Or we have left it to students to take this idea and see where it leads. As is the case with the responses described previously, the text is the starting point—the model for these expansions. The following list includes some possible character transformations to use as discussion or writing prompts:

- Change a character's gender.
- Change a character's age: What would Scout be like as an adult?
- Change the time period: What would Gatsby and his pals be doing at one of his parties in 2011?
- Change the setting: What if the character(s) appeared on *Oprah*?

Advertisements and Recipes in an Author's Style

In this section we explore writing in an author's style in a very different genre. What if famous authors wrote advertising? What would Ken Kesey write about Cocoa Puffs? What if James Joyce wrote an advertisement for the cereal Lucky Charms, "Portrait of the Leprechaun"? Or e. e. cummings celebrated hot dogs, "i wish i were an oscar mayer wiener"? These examples can be found in *Selling Out: If Famous Authors Wrote Advertising* by Joey Green (2011). One of our favorites is "A Tale of Two Deodorants" in the style of Charles Dickens:

> It was the best of smells, it was the worst of smells, it was the age of fragrance, it was the age of stench, it was the epoch of good hygiene, it was the epoch of wretched body odors, it was the season of Cleanliness, it was the season of Perspiration, it was the spring of freshness, it was the summer of vile pungency, we had washed and showered, we were sweating profusely, we were dry and refreshed, we were moist and dank, it was Sure under the left arm, it was the leading deodorant under the right arm—in other words, the comparison was being made between two deodorants, both having been applied simultaneously under opposing arms, and whichever underarm proved direst by day's end would determine which was the superlative product. (75)

Recipes offer another opportunity to explore author style by applying it to a new genre. *Kafka's Soup* by Mark Crick is a delightful collection of recipes in the voices of famous writers. The short form of recipes appeals to students and they seem to enjoy finding connections between food and authors. In the process, they also examine literary craft. We recommend the following recipes from Crick's book as mentors for students: "Quick Miso Soup à la Kafka," "Coq Au Vin à la Gabriel Garcia Marquez," "Mushroom Risotto à la John Steinbeck," and "Tarragon Eggs à la Jane Austen." An excerpt from the Austen recipe is provided here:

4 eggs
1 tablespoon minced fresh tarragon, or 1 teaspoon dried
4 tablespoons butter
Ground pepper
Pinch of salt

It is a truth universally acknowledged that eggs, kept for too long, go off. The eggs of Oakley Farm had only recently been settled in the kitchen at Somecote, but already Mrs. B— was planning a meal that would introduce them to the neighbourhood with what she hoped would be universal acceptance. Her eggs had been strongly endowed by nature with a turn for being uniformly agreeable and she hoped to see at least a half dozen of them make fine matches in the coming week. The arrival of a newcomer in the parish presented the perfect opportunity and Mrs. B— wasted no time in sending out invitations to luncheon. (2005, 10)

Note: Many of these assignments work well during reading as comprehension checks and midway-point analyses.

LITERATURE AS INSPIRATION

To expand on the idea of literature as mentor is to explore a text and then go beyond by creating something new. Students take what they know from reading and analyzing literature and create a literature response in a different genre. The starting point is the text—its structure and craft—but the response is a new creation that expands the student's vision of the original text.

Literary Artifacts

We debated whether these types of "new creation" responses had a term, like *pastiche*, that could help to define them. After some scouring of literary criticism and texts that address writing about literature, we chose to embrace Tom Romano's notion of "literary artifact" to capture the idea of creating a new genre in response to literature. Romano writes:

> **When my students create their own literary artifacts . . . to respond to literature through them, my idea is to celebrate their creative ingenuity, to let them learn about various writing styles and genres from the firsthand experience of making them. I want students to reaffirm their elementary kinship with professional writers, those who view writing not as an ordeal that reveals ineptitude, but as an opportunity to create vision. (1987, 138–139)**

Letters

Students in Kimberly's junior English class were intrigued to read a letter written in May of 1776 from Abigail Smith Adams to her husband, John Adams. Abigail Adams's frustration with John's extended absence from the family is evident. But she also raises issues about the role of women, reminding him that women need to be considered in the new government they are creating. Kimberly asked her students to write a letter to then First Lady Hillary Clinton from Abigail Smith Adams. Imagine what Abigail would write in a letter to Michelle Obama.

After reading *Speak*, sophomore students in Sharon Klin's English class wrote letters to the main character, Melinda. Their empathy and heartfelt advice demonstrated how they had connected with the narrator and her story. Amber wrote this:

> *I think you are a symbol for all of today's teenagers. While most of us have not faced anything quite so horrific as you, you go through many of the same day-to-day problems, especially with relationships. I think there are very few people who have not at one time or another felt left out, mad at a teacher, or had an argument with their parents.*
>
> *In the end I would like to remind you to stay strong and do your best in whatever you would like to do from now on because everything is behind now, even the glass shards.*

And Tim wrote,

We all saw ourselves, each one of us differently every day, as you. We were all Melindas as we swept through the pages of your life story.

Character Journal Entries

Character journal entries allow students to take on the persona of a character by writing journal entries that reflect the character's issues and concerns based on specific events in the text. We have invited students to choose a character and write journal entries as they read a text. We have seen a number of students embrace the character they played during the tea-party strategy (see description in Chapter 3 and examples in Appendix B4). We have also assigned students to write as specific characters. And we have had students write to each other in the role of characters. We are always mindful of the importance of reminding students that the goal of this writing is to further explore the character in the text, so their work must be grounded in their close reading of the text.

Character Facebook Pages

Another way to explore character and encourage the use of technology is through the creation of a Facebook page for a character. We have seen this strategy used effectively with classic as well as more current literature. Picture a Romeo or Juliet Facebook page. What would he or she include? What would each list for his or her status? What would each post on his or her wall? What about the three narrators in *A Yellow Raft in Blue Water* by Michael Dorris? What would each of them put in a Facebook page? We recommend *Ophelia Joined the Group Maidens Who Don't Float: Classic Lit Signs On to Facebook* (Schmelling 2009). This book explores more than fifty authors, including Homer, Twain, and Shakespeare, as if they went online.

Character Conversations Across Texts and/or Time

Kimberly invited her juniors to demonstrate their understanding of the work of poets Emily Dickinson and Walt Whitman by inviting them to write a conversation between the two poets:

You've been immersed in the words of Emily and Walt—two poets who changed the way poetry is written. They were very different in their poetry and the way they lived their lives. I often wonder what they might have said to each other. Join me in this wondering by drafting a conversation between Emily and Walt about poetry. The goal of this conversation is to demonstrate your understanding of these two poets and the writing craft of poetry. To support you in this effort I ask that you identify a poem each poet would bring to a get-together to discuss. Think about what questions they would ask each other. What would they highlight regarding their craft as poets? What response would they have to the other's work? What advice might they share regarding poetry?

Teacher Nicola Onnis built on this idea in creating a final exam question for her American literature class that explored what characters from the literary time periods might say to each other:

A Puritan, a Rationalist, and a Romanticist walk into a café . . .

Your final for Junior English A is to demonstrate your knowledge of the last three units we have covered in American literature by inventing a conversation between three individuals from the three different literary movements. They have traveled through time and are all now seated in a café. Your job is to create a conversation (it may be written in dialogue like a play or told like a story) that covers the following topics for each member of the literary movement:

· *What would they bring to the café to read and why would they make this choice?*

· *How would the three individuals define a hero? How are their definitions different and how are they similar?*

· *What are three different locations where the three believe a person can find the truth and other answers about life? Why do they hold these beliefs about where to find truth?*

· *What core beliefs from their respective literary movements does each individual subscribe to the most, and what historical events caused them to believe in this movement?*

· *On what subject will your three individuals argue or disagree? Your conversation must include one argument between the three members at the café.*

The final grading rubric Nicola used for this final exam is in Appendix F2.

In a unit on Naturalism, a junior chose to write a conversation between "the man" from Jack London's short story "To Build a Fire" and Christopher McCandless, the top student and athlete whose story of trying to survive in Alaska is detailed in Jon Krakauer's book *Into the Wild*. The two characters talked about their journeys into nature and the role of wealth in their lives. Using a screenplay format, the student captured the conversation these two men might have about nature, survival, bad choices and bad luck, and their contrasting views of wealth.

Eulogies for Characters

In addition to reading and writing nonfiction eulogies, we have invited students to write eulogies for fictional characters who die. For example, a eulogy for Gatsby: he creates a personality to present to the world, but what of the real Gatsby? Which Gatsby would students choose to eulogize?

Another use of fictional eulogies is to have students write a eulogy for a character from the point of view of another character. What would Nick write in his eulogy for Gatsby? Kristi has used this effectively with *The Awakening* by having students pick a character and then write a eulogy for Edna Pontellier from the character's point of view. As support for this writing, students can read sample eulogies (see the discussion of eulogies in the "Literature as Mentor" section). Depending on the class, we have assigned students characters from whose point of view they will write the eulogy as well as allowed them to choose, making sure all of the main characters are represented.

Poem in Response to an Essay, Memoir, or Short Story

In Chapter 3, we shared the use of haiku to illustrate plot summary. We have also had students choose to write poetry in response to literature. Kristi has had success asking students to use a text to write a "found poem." Students thumbed through a novel (this lesson worked with *The House on Mango Street* by Sandra Cisneros and *Chronicle of a Death Foretold* by Gabriel Garcia Marquez) and randomly chose ten "powerful" words (words like *a*, *an*, and *the* are not "powerful"). Then they wrote a ten- to fifteen-line poem, including these words and adding in their own transitions and connector words. When this was used as a low-stakes writing assignment during the reading of the text, students were able to grasp the implications of the writers' craft in new ways. As they analyzed the types of words that came up in multiple poems, they were able to address and understand not only style, but also theme, tone, and characterization in new ways.

Putting Characters or the Book on Trial

Throughout Kristi's *Heart of Darkness* unit, students complained and complained. They disliked Conrad's style, could not relate to his characters, and had little to say during discussion. In retrospect, she realizes she did not set students up very well to understand the book, but instead of bemoaning her lack of structure, she decided to create an innovative assignment, putting the book on trial. She wrote the assignment to determine if it was possible to adopt a character's persona and quote the text, yet still offer an opinion about the book. Both years that she did this assignment the attorneys came to class with suits and briefcases, and both times Kurtz's intended had no opinion of her own to offer and thus proved a very difficult witness to question.

The students had fun with a bleak text, and the trial added an element of performance to the year's novel-heavy curriculum. (See Appendix F3, "Assignment for Trial of *Heart of Darkness*," for the detailed assignment and roles.)

We want to clarify that this assignment was a direct response to students' opinions of and reactions to the text. This was not part of Kristi's backward planning for the unit. She learned quickly that this change to her plan had several pros and cons. The pros: students' reactions, even negative feelings about the literature, were valued and guided instruction; students' creative responses enabled them to "own" the literature; and students gained more respect for the writer they had disdained when forced to adopt that writer's style. The cons: a spontaneous assignment can prove difficult to assess; some students, perhaps because they were accustomed to predictable essays, did not take a creative assignment seriously and threw their responses together at the last minute; and one student admitted to having been able to write the final assessment for *Heart of Darkness* without having read the text for detail (this is not to say he earned a respectable grade). This candid student response is a reminder of our note regarding assessment in the introduction to this chapter: summative writing assignments need clear rubrics and/or evaluation criteria to help students and teachers determine how students will demonstrate not just their creativity, but their knowledge of a text. Before Kristi puts *Heart of Darkness* on trial again, she will create specific assessment criteria. But we also want to note that students' sense of ownership of this book is a result of this opportunity to cross-examine the text.

A Graphic Response
It is exciting to see the inclusion of graphic novels in middle school and high school classrooms, including *Maus* (Spiegelman 1986) and *Persepolis* (Satrapi 2003). We also have used graphic novel versions of classic literature in support of students' reading of literature (see the discussion in Chapter 3). We appreciate the use of this genre as a response to literature. We have seen a student write and illustrate a graphic version of *Beowulf*, set in the original as well as a modern setting. Students have also demonstrated their understanding of plot by drawing the main events of a text in graphic form (see "Comic Strip Plot" in Appendix B10).

This I Believe Business Letters
Again we are grateful to teacher Rachel Pass for this idea. After reading a selection of This I Believe essays, she asked her students to brainstorm topics of things they would like to change in their own lives. She found that these questions supported this brainstorming: What do you really care about? What makes you mad? From their

lists, students identified something they would like to change. They reread This I Believe essays as one example of voice through writing.

But they then turned their attention to another way to share their voice: the business letter. Students read sample business letters and made notes about the format of this genre.

In their journals, they wrote more about their proposed topic and shared their ideas with the class. Examples of arguments in support of their stance as well as their counterarguments were modeled by students on an overhead projector. Students followed this modeling with pair-share work in which one of them strongly agreed and the other strongly disagreed. This allowed them to go into their research stage with some ideas about arguments and counterarguments.

Research came next. Students were required to find at least one written source or to conduct an interview related to their topic. Research also included identifying a person or group to whom they could write about their issue.

Drafting, peer response, and editing resulted in final drafts that were then mailed. If this were a movie, all students would have received letters in reply and would have discovered that a business letter allows their voice to be heard. But the real-world story is that only a few received responses, and these were often form letters. Except for Quinn. He wrote to the director of Oregon Prisoners about his concern that prisoners had access to cable. He questioned how this would support them in rehabilitation. He questioned whether prisoners could even be rehabilitated. And he noted that his home did not have cable, so prisoners should not have this privilege. The director responded to Quinn's concerns, noting that prisoners are still human and that although they may have cable, they have lost most of their other privileges. And he invited Quinn to visit the prison.

Letters to Authors

We have mixed feelings about the idea of having students write letters to authors. We appreciate the way letters serve as a written conversation. Bringing in stationery for students to use in writing their letters reinforces that this is a different type of written response. As one student noted, "It's more friendly." But when it comes to sending the letters students write, we note Laurie Halse Anderson's response at an NCTE presentation to a question regarding letters to authors. While she was polite about the letters she received from all the students in a class, letters that had clearly been assigned, she requested that these letters be bundled together so that she could draft a single response. This was not out of disrespect for the assignment but because she gets so many letters from adolescents who are actually struggling with the issues raised in her books. She wants to devote her time to writing individual responses to these readers.

Parent Interviews

Edward Derby, who teaches in a suburban high school just outside of Portland, Oregon, asks his students to interview their parents about their high school experience. The goal is to use this information to compare and contrast school experiences with the school and characters in *A Separate Peace* by John Knowles. The interviews provide a context that the freshmen readers in his class do not yet have regarding high school. And he has found that this assignment not only adds to the exploration of the text but builds connections with parents. The fact that a number of the parents are also alumni of the high school their children attend adds to discussions of the role of high school in our lives.

Parent interviews could also be used to explore names and neighborhoods in connection with *The House on Mango Street*. We have also seen parent interviews assigned during a study of *Romeo and Juliet*. Freshmen were asked to complete a survey about qualities they would value in a spouse or life partner. They then asked their parents to complete the same survey and then interviewed their parents about the survey responses. Students were both surprised and dismayed by their parents' ideas regarding an ideal spouse for their freshman son or daughter. As they read and discussed the play, students referenced their parent interviews, particularly in response to the scenes in the play that involved parents.

Media in Response to Literature

We recognize students' interest in and use of media. Although we are just beginning to explore the possibilities of media in support of literature response, we have witnessed success with the strategies detailed in this section.

Select a Song (or Playlist) That Supports the Text

Students embrace the opportunity to link music with the literature they read. We appreciate the creation of a playlist to accompany an entire text or specific chapters or scenes. For example, a class of sophomores make individual playlists related to *The Secret Life of Bees* by Sue Monk Kidd. Student teachers Kara McPhillips and Gabrielle Buvinger-Wild worked to create connections between Fitzgerald and the juniors with whom they worked. They framed a soundtrack assignment for *The Great Gatsby*. (See Appendixes F4–F7 for an overview of the assignment, a graphic organizer, a sample they modeled, and the grading rubric.) And in another class, freshmen selected and then presented the songs they chose to represent the relationship between Romeo and Juliet. The written analysis that accompanies a student's playlist or song choice provides evidence of the student's understanding of the text and its connection to the song choices. We will also admit to expanding our own music libraries as a result of these playlists.

Podcasts

In Chapter 3 we discuss the value of podcasts in supporting students' understanding of texts as they read. We are just beginning to explore students creating their own podcasts. These could be polished recordings of a small-group or literary circle discussion of a text. Or students could create a podcast reading of a text with commentary. We embrace the possibilities of this technology identified by Sara Kajder, recipient of the first National Technology Leadership Fellowship in English/ Language Arts:

> **A podcast allows for the creation of the readers' artifacts ranging from authentic book talks to literature circles discussions to digital stories . . . In creating audio content, students are scriptwriting, writing questions to stimulate discussion . . . selecting appropriate venues for publishing their work, and responding to comments submitted by listeners. Here, learners evaluate what to say, consider options, and make choices. Learning rests on these risks. (2007, 221)**

We are new to this use of technology, so we recommend the resources listed in Kajder's chapter in *Adolescent Literacy: Turning Promise into Practice* (2007).

Book Trailers

Drawing on the idea of movie trailers to create an audience for film, a book trailer uses this format to create an audience for a book. Kimberly's son made a book trailer for Ray Bradbury's novel *Something Wicked This Way Comes* for his high school English class. Kristi's colleague Lori Townzen has used this assignment for *King Lear*. We found numerous examples of book trailers on YouTube, including middle school and high school examples. We have heard from several teachers that they use book trailers to help students choose literature circle texts. In some cases, they use the book trailers created by their students. They find having a real audience increases the quality of the trailer. They also use examples they find on YouTube.

Cast a Film Version of a Text with Justification for Character and Setting Choices and/or Create a Movie Poster

We have used this response with literature circle groups as well as with individual student projects. The rationale for students' choices of actors or setting is evidence of their understanding of the text. We have witnessed heated debates about casting decisions regarding who would be best to play "Death" in a film of Emily Dickinson's poem "Because I Could Not Stop for Death" or Holden Caufield in a film version of *The Catcher in the Rye*, a film Hollywood is eager to make. And we note the number of book trailers based on *The Catcher in the Rye* that can be found on YouTube. Sometimes this project leads to the creation of a film based on a book scene or a film pastiche that uses the characters and/or plot of the original text.

Film

After being immersed in the study of Poe and Thoreau in their English class, three juniors created a film to show their understanding and appreciation of these authors. Rather than set the film in the time period of the Romantics, they chose to create a modern-day sitcom starring Poe and Thoreau. Emerson was even included as the next-door neighbor.

Their goal was to contrast the writing styles of Poe and Thoreau by making them mismatched roommates. Thoreau thought everything was wonderful and celebrated nature on his way in and out of the apartment. Poe, on the other hand, was dark and brooding. He sat huddled in a corner writing poetry. When there was a knock upon the door, Poe began reciting "The Raven." Embedded in the humor of this video was evidence of understanding about the unique writing styles of each author and their contributions to American literature.

We have also seen short films created by students in response to novels they have read, such as the re-creation of a scene from Craig Lesley's *Winter Kill* and a talk show based on the characters from *The Bean Trees* by Barbara Kingsolver.

Note: We have learned to require a written statement from each student about how the film reflects his or her understanding of the text. We have learned the hard way that students can create a wonderful re-creation of a scene from a text that they have not fully read.

Video Games

One junior drew on his reading of *The Scarlet Letter* by Nathaniel Hawthorne and his love of video games and created "Lost Dimsdale," a game in which Dimsdale fights his inner demons. Recently we were sent a link to a "video" game based on *The Great*

Gatsby that uses a similar arcade-style game: http://greatgatsbygame.com/.

We have heard from "gamers" that there is a video game based on Dante's *Inferno*: www.dantesinferno.com/. We do note it is an M-rated game, which is the video game equivalent of an R movie rating. Experiencing a text in the form of a video game can enrich student understanding.

*   *   *

It is our hope that in creating the responses described in this chapter, students will come to understand and appreciate the literature that serves as their mentor and/or inspiration. And they will discover that they, too, are writers.

APPENDIX A

1. Introduction Letter

Dear Students, (We have also used the entire class list of students in the salutation or have handwritten names for each individual student.)

Greetings! I am so looking forward to our work together this year. This is my eighth year teaching English 9 at Estacada High School; I also teach English 11 and Leadership. Prior to teaching, I spent several years working as an attorney. I handled a variety of cases, but the most difficult involved juveniles charged with crimes. In fact, it was this work that led me back to teaching. I realized that as teachers we have the opportunity to help students find their voices as readers, writers, and citizens of the world. It's my hope that I can support you in finding your voice.

I grew up in Denver, Colorado, and graduated from Cherry Creek High School. I came to Oregon because I love the rain and wanted to study at Lewis & Clark College, where I earned my BA in English. I then taught middle school English for three years before going to law school at Willamette University College of Law. After leaving law, I returned to Lewis & Clark and earned my master's degree in teaching.

When I am not teaching, I enjoy time with my family. We have two children. John is four and hopes to be a film director or a superhero when he grows up. He is often dressed as a superhero when I arrive home. Kinsey is eighteen months old. She is very talkative and has just learned to run, which is exciting for her and challenging for her parents. I am fortunate to have a husband who stays home to provide full-time care. He is an avid sports fan and enjoys scary movies.

I grew up in Colorado, so I do love to ski, but I rarely get to the mountains to do so. I was a competitive swimmer from the time I was five until college. And I think it's important that you know I am a Denver Broncos fan. I also enjoy watching tennis.

It's probably no surprise that I love to read. But I read a wide variety of books. My current favorite kind of "good read" is murder mysteries. My daughter, Kinsey, is named after a private detective in a murder mystery series written by Sue Grafton. I am also a fan of short stories and so excited that we will be reading this genre as a class. We will spend time every Wednesday reading "choice" books. I look forward to finding out your favorite authors and genres.

In addition to reading choice books, we'll explore a range of literature and will write about the books we read, and you'll have time in writing workshop to discover and develop your own stories.

So please tell me about yourself. How long have you lived in Estacada? Where else have you lived? What should I know about your family? What do you like to do when you are not in school? What do you like to read (feel free to list magazines as well as books)? What should I know about you as a learner?

With downright good cheer,
Mrs. Campbell (If possible, I sign each letter.)

2. Student Survey for the First Week of School

Note: This information will help me to know you as a member of our classroom community. I will not share your answers with anyone without your permission.

Name (please list the name you would like to be called if it is different from your legal name): _____

What are you good at in an English class?

What is something you would like to work on this year in our English class?

What are you looking forward to in our English class this year? What, if anything, are you worried or concerned about?

What should I know about you as a student to help you be successful?

What question do you wish I had asked? I would be grateful if you would answer this question.

What question do you want to ask me?

On the back, please list your typical daily schedule. I know you lead busy lives and I want to be respectful of all your commitments. In particular, note after-school responsibilities such as sports, work, or expectations of your family.

3. Sample Unit Plan

UNIT PLAN FOR *CHRONICLE OF A DEATH FORETOLD* BY GABRIEL GARCIA MARQUEZ

UNIT QUESTIONS
- How does keeping a journal while reading provide evidence for an analytical essay?
- How can we identify a theme and discuss the way it is developed over the course of a novel?
- How do we identify key turning points in a text and articulate why they can be seen as turning points?

OBJECTIVES
What will students know, understand, and be able to do?
- Students will track key passages connected to theme in a novel.
- Students will write about key passages on their way to discovering their own ideas about the themes they choose to track in the novel.
- Students will write an essay based on a key passage, showing what makes that passage key and how it illustrates theme.

How will you know what students know, understand, and are able to do?

- Preassessment (prereading):
  - Analysis of and discussion of first line of novel
  - "Throwing lines" activity (each student receives one quotation from the novel) to analyze key passages, make predictions, and connect to theme
- Ongoing Assessment (during reading):
  - Key passage journal maintained for every night of reading and colored tabs used in the text to track the development of two themes
  - Class discussions and in-class group writing to expand understanding of text
- Postassessment (Postreading)
  - Journals evaluated
  - Key passage essay, three to five pages

How will you support students in their efforts to know, understand, and do? What will you need to teach? Model?
- **Reading: How to select a key passage for a journal**

- Reading: How theme develops
- Writing: How to discuss what makes a key passage "key"
- Writing: How to transform journals and in-class writing into an essay that analyzes a key passage

What activities do you have planned?
- First line and "throwing lines" analyses to model how to identify and discuss key passages
- Daily journal sharing and discussion
- Socratic seminar to develop analysis
- Group-created thesis statements and "one-pagers"
- Mini-lessons
  - Review: color-coding passages
  - Drafting the key passage essays (mini-lessons in response to student drafting)

What materials and resources will you use?
- Student journals
- The novel *Chronicle of a Death Foretold*
- Teacher-created mini-lessons, bookmarks, and discussion questions

APPENDIX B

1. Sample Anticipation Guides

The Awakening by Kate Chopin
Based on your own opinion and experiences in the world, label the following statements true or false, and then explain your answer.

1. T   F   It is important to marry for love.

_____
_____
_____
_____

2. T   F   People who have money have more freedom than people who are poor.

_____
_____
_____
_____

3. T   F   A mother's first responsibility is her children.

_____
_____
_____
_____

4. T   F   Creating or taking time to appreciate some form of art is crucial to maintaining happiness.

_____
_____
_____
_____

5. T   F   Until someone knows himself or herself, he or she can never be truly happy.

_____

_____

_____

_____

6. T   F   Finding personal satisfaction is more important than making others happy.

_____

_____

_____

_____

Song of Solomon by Toni Morrison

Based on your own opinion and experiences in the world, label the following statements true or false, and then explain your answer.

1. T   F   It is important to know and understand your family's heritage.

_____

_____

_____

2. T   F   We are all products of our environment.

_____

_____

_____

3. T   F   A person's race affects who his or her friends are.

_____

_____

_____

4. T   F   A person's socioeconomic class (e.g., wealthy, impoverished, working class, etc.) affects who his or her friends are.

_____

_____

_____

_____

5. T   F   A person's race affects the position/social standing he or she can have in his or her community.

_____

_____

_____

_____

6. T   F   A person's socioeconomic class affects the position/social standing he or she can have in his or her community.

_____

_____

_____

_____

7. T   F   It is easy for a person to know who he or she is.

_____

_____

_____

_____

8. T   F   A person's name affects who he or she is.

_____

_____

_____

_____

9.   T   F   Novels should have an easy-to-follow, linear plot.

_____

_____

_____

_____

10.   T   F   High school students are too old to read fairy tales or folk tales.

_____

_____

_____

_____

11.   T   F   People can fly.

_____

_____

_____

_____

2. First Impressions (or, Judging a Book by Its Cover)

Book Title:

Author:

LIST OF THINGS I NOTICE ABOUT THIS BOOK BASED ON THE FRONT AND BACK COVER.	WHAT I THINK ABOUT THE THINGS I NOTICED.
Synthesize: Reread your list and thoughts. Make a few statements about this book based on what you noticed.	

3. Second Impressions (or, Judging a Book by What's Between the Covers)

Book Title:

Author:

LIST OF THINGS I NOTICE ABOUT THIS BOOK BASED ON WHAT'S BETWEEN THE COVERS.	WHAT I THINK ABOUT THE THINGS I NOTICED.
Synthesize: Reread your list and thoughts. Make a few statements about this book based on what you noticed.	

4. Character Tea Party for *The Breadwinner* by Deborah Ellis

Character Lists

Part A

Directions: As you meet each character, write down his/her name and answer the following questions about his/her life.

1. Find someone who was fired from her job because she is a woman. How does she feel about her life now?
Character:

2. Find someone who lost the lower part of his leg in an explosion at his school. Who helps him get where he needs to go?
Character:

3. Find someone who doesn't remember a time when there weren't bombs exploding outside her house. How does she help her family?
Character:

4. Find someone who can secretly read and write. What's her favorite subject?
Character:

5. Find someone who has an annoying little sister. Why is her sister jealous of her?
Character:

6. Find someone who wants to start a secret school. What did she win a medal for?
Character:

7. Find someone who has a boy's name. What is it? Why did she have to start working outside her house?

Character:

Part B

My Questions: After meeting all of the characters, write at least four questions about things you want to find out more about as you read (about the characters or the book in general).

1. _____
2. _____
3. _____
4. _____

Part C

Draw a diagram, symbol, graph, tree, or picture that shows how you think the characters are connected/related.

Explain your drawing:_____
_____
_____
_____

Part D

What predictions do you have about *The Breadwinner* and/or the characters? Write at least three.

1. _____
2. _____
3. _____

Character Statements for *The Breadwinner*

Mother

I have a university degree and I used to work as a writer for a radio station in Kabul before the Taliban took over. I also used to be part of the Afghan Women's Union and spoke out for women's rights. I was not afraid to voice my opinion about politics.

Since the Taliban came, life has been much harder for me. I was fired from my job at the radio station because I am a woman. Now, I cannot go outside without the company of a man. I haven't left my house in a year.

I have three daughters and a son. I have another son, Hossain, who was killed in a land mine explosion a few years ago. Although I am a strong person, I am heartbroken about Hossain's death.

Father

I have three daughters and two sons—one of whom was killed a few years ago in a land mine explosion. Even though I have faced hard times, I still have a sense of humor and try to see the good in things. I used to be a history teacher before the Taliban took over. I went to school in England, where I grew to love reading and books.

Several years ago, the high school I was teaching in was bombed, and I lost the lower part of my leg. My daughter Parvana helps me walk and get where I need to go. I am grateful to be married to a smart and confident woman, Fatana. I have always supported women's education and am frustrated at how women are forbidden to go to school under the Taliban.

Maryam

I am Parvana's youngest sister. I am only five years old. I live with my mother, father, brother, and two sisters in a small, one-roomed house. We used to live in a bigger house, but it was bombed and we had to move. I don't really remember a time when there weren't bombs exploding outside my front door.

I love my sister Parvana very much, even though she thinks I am a chatterbox. I try to help her out whenever I can. I also like to help my family by playing with my youngest brother, Ali. He is just a baby.

Parvana

History was my favorite subject when I could go to school. My country's been at war all my life. I'm only in sixth grade but I live in Afghanistan, so I have to hide much of my life. No one is supposed to know, but I can read and write. Sometimes I'm scared but I have to help my family even though I don't think I look like a boy. What would happen if I didn't go out and work, buy food, and fetch water?

Nooria

Parvana is so annoying. She's jealous of my long, thick hair. Maybe when you're in high school, all sixth-grade little sisters are annoying. How long do they expect us to stay inside? Just because I'm a woman I can't go outside? I don't even want to think about how long it's been since I've been to school. I help Mother clean and take care of my baby brother, Ali, and five-year-old sister, Maryam.

Mrs. Weera

I miss being around kids; I miss being a PE teacher. I know my hair is white, but my body is strong. The Taliban doesn't think women should be out of the house so I lost my job. I still have my medal, though. I was once the fastest woman runner in Afghanistan.

I know Parvana doesn't like the idea, but it's our best option to have food and stay alive. I was glad to help Fatana and her children. All of us living together, including my granddaughter, works out well for everyone, and Fatana and I can start our own magazine. I want to start a secret school, too.

Shauzia

I'd been working as a tea boy for six months before I saw Parvana from my class. She really hadn't been my friend, but I was happy to see someone from school. I told her my boy name, Shafiq. I had to go to work when my father died of a bad heart.

Maybe Parvana (Kaseem) and I can work together at the market. I hope Mrs. Weera will start her secret school so I can learn. We have to live with my father's parents and they don't think I should know how to read and write. I have to get out.

5. *The Great Gatsby* Launch Party—Who's Who?

CHARACTER	TWO INTERESTING FACTS ABOUT THIS CHARACTER	YOUR RELATIONSHIP TO THIS CHARACTER
Jay Gatsby	1. 2.	
Nick Carraway	1. 2.	
Daisy Buchanan	1. 2.	
Tom Buchanan	1. 2.	
Jordan Baker	1. 2.	
Myrtle Wilson	1. 2.	
George Wilson	1. 2.	

Jay Gatsby
You probably haven't met me, but anybody who's anybody comes to my huge parties. I live in a giant mansion, drive the most expensive cars, and wear the finest custom suits. Don't tell anyone, but I haven't always been rich. I had to make my own fortune to impress a girl. Not just any girl—the most beautiful girl you've ever seen: Daisy Buchanan. We dated while I was in the military, but she wouldn't marry me because I was poor. That's when I decided I had to get rich, even if it meant breaking the law. I heard that Daisy married some clown named Tom. I bought my mansion near theirs and have been hanging around her cousin, Nick, so that I can see her again. I just know I can win her back.

Jordan Baker
Listen, a little white lie here and there never hurt anyone. I mean, it's the twenties, and a girl's gotta do what she can to get ahead. Like me, for instance. So what if I fibbed to win my first golf tournament? If I hadn't done that I'd never get the opportunity to travel around as a pro golfer, meeting exciting new friends like Tom and Daisy, going to all the fun parties that happen in New York, like the ones that Jay Gatsby throws. Those are the best. I'm young, cute, and a bit of a tomboy, just what all the guys are after these days. Well, all of them except Nick. We've been dating a bit, but I can't seem to pin him down.

Daisy Buchanan
I grew up in a huge house with everything that I could possible want. I have never had a shortage of friends or boyfriends because I am incredibly beautiful and fun to be around. Most people would probably say that my life is pretty easy; they don't know about my problems. My husband is Tom Buchanan. He is tall and handsome, but he has been cheating on me for a long time with another woman. I had a lover when I was younger, but he did not have enough money to marry me. I got tired of waiting; that is when I married Tom. Now my old lover is back in my life, and I have realized that I still love him. I don't know what to do. Should I leave my husband? As if all of this were not bad enough, I killed someone.

Tom Buchanan
I guess that you might call my family rich; I guess that you might call me rich for that matter. I was a college sports star for a while, but I got tired of all of that. I am used to getting what I want when I want it. I get the money that I want, the cars that I want, and the women that I want. Take my wife, Daisy, for instance, she is beautiful and funny, and she comes from a good family. I knew as soon as I met her that I wanted to marry her, so

I did. I met Daisy through her cousin Nick Carraway when we went to college together. Married life bores me sometimes though, so I have a girlfriend named Myrtle Wilson on the side. I think that this is perfectly normal for a man to have someone on the side, but I would be furious if Daisy ever cheated on me. I am athletic and love going to the country club to play golf, which, I am happy to say, does not allow any colored people.

Myrtle Wilson

Life has not been good to me. I should have married a rich man who could give me everything that I wanted, but instead I ended up with a dull auto mechanic named George Wilson. We lived in a tiny boring town upstairs from the garage and I had to put up with his constant talk about cars. I knew that I deserved better, and that's where Tom Buchanan came in. Tom saw me for who I really was. He treated me like a lady. He rented an apartment for me in the city and bought me dresses and furs. I just know that one day he would have left his wife for me, but unfortunately someone killed me before he had the chance.

George Wilson

I might not be the best looking or smartest man, but I am a good mechanic and a good husband. Unfortunately, my wife, Myrtle, doesn't like me very much; she thinks that I am too slow and too poor. She liked me fine when we got married, but she gets bored pretty quickly. She has been going to the city a lot lately; sometimes she even spends the night. She claims that she is visiting her sister, but I am starting to think that she might be seeing someone else. This makes me so mad that I could just kill someone.

Nick Carraway

I came to New York after college to learn the bond business, but I've been learning a heck of a lot more than that. My cousin, Daisy, lives here with her husband, Tom. I'm not sure about him—he cheats on Daisy with a woman from the city. And their friend Jordan, she's an unusual woman, wearing pants and traveling all about the country alone. Then there's my neighbor, Jay Gatsby. He's rich beyond compare, and throws over-the-top parties every Saturday night. I'm not sure how he got his money; he's very mysterious and secretive. But one secret he has shared is the fact that he's in love with my cousin, Daisy. I guess they had a fling when they were kids. He wants my help winning her back. I'm all mixed up in the middle of things. It seems like everyone out here just parties and has affairs! It's not like that back in Minnesota. But, I try not to judge. As my dad always says, "Whenever you feel like criticizing someone, remember that they haven't had all the advantages that you've had."

6. Slide-Show Student Instructions

1. *With your group, review your assigned section and decide on the five to seven most important moments. Everyone should write them down (paraphrasing is fine). For example: When Scout and Jem find Dill under the bed. Choose one narrator. This will be the person reading the voice-over during your presentation. Cast characters for each of the moments. Make a list of all the characters who show up in your slides.*

2. *Decide who is going to play each character. If you need to double up (i.e., have one student play more than one character), please make sure each character has a small role and that it is easy for your audience to distinguish the character change (think new costumes or name tags). If you have too many people and not enough characters, have someone be an inanimate object, like a tree.*

3. *Do a quick sketch of each slide. Include the set (for example, the swing could be three chairs pushed together) and where each character will stand. As long as you are quiet in the halls and/or clear it with another teacher, you can use most of the school as a set (perhaps even use the outside).*

4. *Write a voice-over of each slide. You must paraphrase what was written in the book. Have each voice-over be at least three, but no more than six, sentences. Make sure your script is legible for most people. If you want to type it up, go ahead.*

5. *Make any set pieces (for example, a tree out of butcher paper), props, and costumes (or make a list of what people need to bring from home).*

7. Slide-Show Graphic Organizer

Slide #:
Location of photo shoot:
Characters/actors:
Costumes:
Props:
Set pieces:
Voice-over script:
Sketch the scene on the back of this paper.

Beyond the Five-Paragraph Essay by Kimberly Hill Campbell and Kristi Latimer. Copyright © 2012. Stenhouse Publishers.

8. Haiku Summary Student Instructions

As a class we will rewrite a section of the book through haiku.

1.   *Write two haikus per chapter assigned.*
2.   *In class, rewrite each haiku onto a separate slip of paper or a sticky note.*
3.   *Take your haikus and get with a partner.*
4.   *Using creativity, logic, and imagination, put your haikus in chronological order.*
5.   *After doing this with a partner, find another partner pair and do it again (now you're working with four sets of haikus).*
6.   *Do this until the entire class has become one group and all the haikus are in chronological order.*
7.   *Put haikus in order on the wall in the hall.*

Please note that you are synthesizing, the highest level of thinking in Bloom's Taxonomy. This is a messy process and does not have an exact "correct" answer. What is important about this activity is the thinking that you are doing during the process. Exercise your brain and make order out of chaos!

9. Plot, Theme, and Symbol Bookmarks

READING FOR PLOT	READING FOR PLOT	READING FOR PLOT
Important Event:	Important Event:	Important Event:
Supporting Quote (w/page #):	Supporting Quote (w/page #):	Supporting Quote (w/page #):
Important Event:	Important Event:	Important Event:
Supporting Quote (w/page #):	Supporting Quote (w/page #):	Supporting Quote (w/page #):
Important Event:	Important Event:	Important Event:
Supporting Quote (w/page #):	Supporting Quote (w/page #):	Supporting Quote (w/page #):
Important Event:	Important Event:	Important Event:
Supporting Quote (w/page #):	Supporting Quote (w/page #):	Supporting Quote (w/page #):

Beyond the Five-Paragraph Essay by Kimberly Hill Campbell and Kristi Latimer. Copyright © 2012. Stenhouse Publishers.

READING FOR THEME	**READING FOR THEME**	**READING FOR THEME**
Theme:	Theme:	Theme:
Supporting Quote (w/page #):	Supporting Quote (w/page #):	Supporting Quote (w/page #):
Supporting Quote (w/page #):	Supporting Quote (w/page #):	Supporting Quote (w/page #):
Supporting Quote (w/page #):	Supporting Quote (w/page #):	Supporting Quote (w/page #):
Theme:	Theme:	Theme:
Supporting Quote (w/page #):	Supporting Quote (w/page #):	Supporting Quote (w/page #):
Supporting Quote (w/page #):	Supporting Quote (w/page #):	Supporting Quote (w/page #):
Supporting Quote (w/page #):	Supporting Quote (w/page #):	Supporting Quote (w/page #):

READING FOR SYMBOLISM	READING FOR SYMBOLISM	READING FOR SYMBOLISM
Symbol:	Symbol:	Symbol:
Supporting Quote (w/page #):	Supporting Quote (w/page #):	Supporting Quote (w/page #):
Supporting Quote (w/page #):	Supporting Quote (w/page #):	Supporting Quote (w/page #):
Supporting Quote (w/page #):	Supporting Quote (w/page #):	Supporting Quote (w/page #):
Symbol:	Symbol:	Symbol:
Supporting Quote (w/page #):	Supporting Quote (w/page #):	Supporting Quote (w/page #):
Supporting Quote (w/page #):	Supporting Quote (w/page #):	Supporting Quote (w/page #):
Supporting Quote (w/page #):	Supporting Quote (w/page #):	Supporting Quote (w/page #):

10. Comic Strip Plot

What happened first?	What happened next?	What happened last?
Cartoon	Cartoon	Cartoon

APPENDIX C

1. Key Passage Analysis Journal Guidelines

Quote: Write out a passage that seems "key," or important, to you:
Summarize: What does the passage *say*?
Analyze, Step 1: What might the passage *mean*? What questions arise for you when you read it?
Analyze, Step 2: How does the author convey meaning? What techniques do you notice? Remember, every passage has tone, diction, and syntax.
Connect/Compare/Contrast: How does the passage connect to other important passages/moments in the text?
Evaluate: What, ultimately, are we to learn from the author?

2. Three-Part Journal Sample Requirements and Sample Entry

Things Fall Apart by Chinua Achebe

In your reading notebook, you will record your reactions to each novel. Pay particular attention to interesting quotations, and allow yourself to question the text. Your journals for *Things Fall Apart* will be three-part entries. They must consist of at least one page of writing. Remember: Your journal is a place for your initial ideas and explorations. Do not feel that you must write flawless analysis or have a mini-thesis for every entry. Do feel that you must think and engage with the text while you read.

Journal Part 1: Summary
Include at least three bullet points of summary. What happens in the chapter? Who do we meet? What actions are taken? You may write these as you read or when you finish the chapter.

Journal Part 2: Golden Lines
You must quote at least three lines (or groups of lines) from the text. What makes a line "golden," you ask? A golden line can be a beautiful piece of imagery, a turning point for a character, a striking bit of dialogue, or a moment that surprises you. Choose lines that allow you to appreciate Achebe's style.

Journal Part 3: Evaluative Question
I record questions in my journal as I read. You may do the same, but choose one and attempt to answer it thoughtfully. This is the end of the journal and the place where you will do your independent analysis. An "evaluative" question forces you to evaluate something about the book. It should take at least two paragraphs to address. Consider literary elements like character motivation, setting, conflict, dialogue, minor characters, proverbs, and so on. A strong example of an evaluative question is "What will be the result of Okonkwo's preoccupation with masculinity?" A bad example of an evaluative question is "How did Okonkwo become so manly?" You must think and predict to answer the former; the latter is answered for you, so your answer will merely summarize the text.

See the sample entry on the back.

Things Fall Apart, pgs. 1–36

Summary:
Introduction of Okonkwo; he threw the Cat
Ikemefuna brought to village as compensation for the killing of an Ibo woman;
Ikemefuna's story "still told today."
Okonkwo built his farm by himself because his father left him nothing.
Okonkwo was punished for beating his wife during the Week of Peace.

Golden Lines
"And so on this particular night as the crier's voice was gradually swallowed up in the distance, silence returned to the world, a vibrant silence made more intense by the universal trill of a million million forest insects." (13)
"Okonkwo was ruled by one passion—to hate everything that his father Unoka had loved. One of these things was gentleness and another was idleness." (17)
"A proud heart can survive a general failure because such a failure does not prick its pride. It is more difficult and more bitter when a man fails *alone*." (27)

Evaluative Question
In what ways do the Ibo people attempt to control nature? When do they acknowledge that nature is beyond their control?

I'm thinking about this because of Unoka's chasing of and respect of the kite in the first chapter. He finds joy in music, in creating music, but seems resistant to applying that joy to tribal ceremony. He does not seem to respect the traditions of the tribe (repaying debts, planting a robust farm, caring for his family), but he does honor nature. If he contrasts so sharply with Okonkwo and Okonkwo seeks to control nature (working diligently for his yam crop), which is the "right" way to be? What is Achebe trying to teach us about controlling vs. appreciating nature? Is there a balance to be sought?

The ending of Chapter 4 focuses on the all-powerful rain and even suggests that the village rainmaker should not attempt to alter the rain's patterns during periods of extreme dryness or powerful storms. Even holy men know their limits; the rain's forces would damage the man's health and were "far too great for the human frame" (35). How do the Ibo decide when to relinquish control? When can they influence the world around them, and when must they attribute natural events to the gods?

3. Bookmark-Guided Journal Sample

Note for clarification: We have used bookmarks, including the one below, to ensure that students have their ongoing requirements at hand while they read. On one side, we print the reading instructions. On the other side, we add details pertinent to the particular text and/or journal assignment. For example, the journal below is printed with a character list on the reverse side. We have also printed model journals on one side, or lists of questions, or quotations to watch for. The possibilities are endless and can be adjusted to enhance any unit plan.

Reading Instructions for *Chronicle of a Death Foretold* by Gabriel Garcia Marquez

Please consult your class calendar for the daily reading assignments. As always, you may read beyond the assigned chapters, but at a minimum you should read the chapters indicated on the calendar by the beginning of class on the designated day. Each day, you will come to class with a journal written in response to the homework reading. Your journal will be a key passage journal analyzing one passage from the chapter that illustrates one of the key concepts outlined below. You will perform a mini-commentary (analyze style) on the passage for a paragraph, then connect it with the rest of the novel/chapter for the rest of a full page of writing.

Daily journals should address the presence and the development of *your choice* of the following key concepts:

- *Memory* — explain its elusive nature and how it affects storytelling
- *Animal Imagery* — connect to characterization and theme
- *Narrator's Role* — explain how the narrator's reliability impacts the story
- *Religion* — focus on the difference between practice and belief
- *Social Class* — discuss class's effect on characters' actions and reputations
- *Irony* — analyze why irony is crucial to this particular story
- *Gender Roles* — no explanation needed

4. List Journal Sample

Journal 4   130-190

- "It was then, in the presence of that personality which was offensive to her, that the woman, by her divine art, seemed to reach Edna's spirit and set it free" (131).
- "And she would seat herself at the piano and play as her humor prompted her while the young woman read the letter" (133)
- "She sat holding it in her hand, while the music penetrated her whole being like an effulgence, warming and brightening the dark places of her soul. It prepared her for joy and exultation" (134)
- "Are you in love with Robert?" "Yes," said Edna. It was the first time she had admitted it, and a glow overspread her face, blotching it with red spots" (135)
- "It was the first kiss of her life to which her nature had really responded. It was a flaming torch that kindled desire" (139)
- "What about the dinner?" he asked; "the grand event, the coup d'etate?" (142)
- "Monsieur Ratignolle stared a little, and turned to ask Mademoiselle Reisz if she considered the symphony concerts up to the standard which had been set the previous winter" (146-147)
- "Then, looking at Edna, he began to sing; "Ah! si tu savais!" (150)
- "A profound stillness had fallen upon the broad, beautiful street. The voices of Edna's disbanding guests jarred like a discordant note upon the quiet harmony of the night" (151)
- "Yes, and chilled, and miserable. I feel so if I had been wound up to a certain pitch - too tight - and something inside of me had snapped" (153)

At this point in the book, Edna has fully realized that she is unhappy with her life, hence her purchasing her own house. The interesting thing about this section is that Mr. Pontellier is notably passive. Although he did tactfully do some remodeling to make it look like Edna had to move, if he *really* cared he would have come back and tried to reconcile with his wife. As for music, Edna is changing by the music making her realize her unhappiness. She says "I feel as if I had been wound up to a certain pitch- too tight- and something inside of me had snapped." (153). At this point, she has realized that she is so unhappy and doesn't really want to keep on living this way.

APPENDIX D

1. Sample Formal Journal

Huck's Storytellin' and Other Such Truck

Huck's lies/stories/conversations with Jim and the silences between them have intrigued me throughout this reading of *Adventures of Huckleberry Finn*. When forced to be honest, Huck turns to Jim, with whom he shares a common language—no need to interpret riddles (posed by Buck) or clamor through self-serving nonsense (King and Duke). As Huck transitions from Tom Sawyer's protégé in adventures inspired by novels and tall tales to an independent boy negotiating a complex world, he experiences real-life situations that call into question Tom's prescriptions for "robbing and killing." Buck's death leaves Huck speechless; he has no appropriate method to tell the story of Buck's death. The only language he has to describe risk and adventure is Tom's, and Tom's language is woefully inadequate and, Huck seems to begin to recognize, trivial.

The Duke and the King appear shortly after Huck leaves the Grangerfords. The King's butchering of *Hamlet* represents another moment when canonical language and literature fail the purposes of Huck's journey. Above all else, the King and the Duke are storytellers. When the King attempts the "to be or not to be" speech, he mixes Hamlet's language with bits of *Macbeth*. To some extent Twain mocks the consumers of traditional education (Emmeline and her poetry within the Grangerford's book-filled home and absurd feud; Tom and his ridiculous demands), but with the King, Twain seems to revere the language, noting that someone as depraved as the King would merely pervert the complex moral debate of the "to be or not to be" speech.

When Huck first dresses up as Sarah Mary Williams, Jim corrects his walk and voice in order to help him act more believably like a girl. Huck replies, "I listened. And I done better." That one line captures an essential component of Huck's character: he listens to other people's stories and sees their corruptions specifically so that he can tell a better story—his own.

2. Journal Assignment for *To Kill a Mockingbird*

We're doing something different with your journal assignment—you're going to have time to write them in class. For each homework reading, please choose one (and it can be a different one every time) of the following response methods to use:

- *Key Passages*: **Pick a piece of text from the reading and comment on it. Explain why it struck you and how it relates to the book as a whole.**
- *Personal Connection*: **Explain a personal connection you have to an event/character/theme in the novel.**
- *Literary Connection*: **Explain a connection you've noticed between this novel and another text you have read.**
- *World Connection*: **Explain a connection you've noticed between this novel and contemporary or historical events/issues.**
- *Question & Answer*: **Develop a "dense" question about what you've read and try to answer it.**

In responding, use one or several of the literary terms you have learned over the last two years to describe the structural/thematic/character elements you address in your response.

Although you'll have time in class to write, that doesn't let you off when you're doing your reading. You'll need to *prepare*: as you read, keep an eye to what type of response you will want to write during class. Use the sticky notes we've provided (Yeah! We're giving you sticky notes! Yeah!) to mark passages or questions or ideas that you'll want to address in class.

3. Personal Commentary Question Proposal

We're coming closer to the end of the novel, and as we have talked about before, we will be using our log assignment entries as the building blocks of the personal commentary that we will be writing in response to a question we have about *Mockingbird*. In support of this and as a pre-spring-break assessment, please complete the following assignment:

1. *Propose a question about Mockingbird that you would like to respond to for your personal commentary. This can be a question you have already asked in your writing or one that we have already asked in class.*
2. *Read over your log assignment entries so far.*
3. *Identify those entries or parts of entries (including key passages) that you feel address this question, or that you feel represent some strong thinking.*
4. *Type up your question and the entries or parts of entries you selected.*
5. *At the end of this, please describe the direction you plan to go with your personal commentary. Briefly tell me the story of how you will answer your question.*

This assignment must be typed, and it should not take you too long. You have been doing the real hard work when you wrote every day in class. Make sure, however, that you are thoughtful putting this together; you will use it as the basis for your personal commentary.

The assignment will be assessed based on the quality of your question (remember the traits of good questions we talked about), the thoughtfulness and appropriateness of your selected journal entries, and the clarity of your described plan.

APPENDIX E

1. Incorporating Quotation Practice

Song of Solomon by Toni Morrison

Each quotation in an essay must be clearly introduced and analyzed.

An introduction should identify one or several of the following:

+ *Who* is speaking?
+ *Where* do the events described take place? OR *Where* does the quotation appear in the text?
+ *When* does this quotation appear in the text? OR *When* does the character say it? Before or after a major event? At a turning point in his/her life?

An analysis can come before the quotation, but most often follows it. The analysis should always answer the following questions:

+ *Why* are these lines important enough to quote?
+ *What* do we learn, *beyond plot summary*, from this quotation?
+ *How* does quoting these lines enhance your argument?

The following are several examples of quotations that lack introduction or appropriate analysis. Some also contain formatting errors. On the lines provided, briefly explain what is done right and what is wrong.

1. *Milkman and Guitar arrive at Mary's bar to talk: "It was empty at eight-thirty in the evening, when Guitar and Milkman arrived" (84).*

_____

_____

_____

_____

2. *Guitar discusses his prowess as a hunter. "'I was never scared—not of the dark or shadows or funny sounds, and I was never afraid to kill. Anything.'" (85) Guitar's lack of fear and the emphasis on the word "anything" suggest that Guitar may have a propensity for violence.*

_____

_____

_____

_____

3. *Milkman is deformed. "By the time Milkman was fourteen he had noticed that one of his legs was shorter than the other" (62). Milkman has no confidence in himself and so imagines that his deformity is worse than it is.*

_____

_____

_____

_____

4. *"[T]heir generosity was so whole-hearted it looked like carelessness," (92). Morrison discusses gender roles and that women are expected to be giving.*

_____

_____

_____

_____

YOUR TURN TO WRITE!

The following quotations are from Chapter 4. Introduce and analyze them in relation to one of the key ideas listed in the journal.

1. "'Was that something? Wow! She's two inches taller than he is, and she's talking about weak.'
   'We are weak.'
   'Compared to what? A B-52?'" (96)

2. "'There are all kinds of people in this world. Some are curious, some ain't; some talk, some scream; some are kickers and other people are kicked. Take your daddy, now. He's a kicker.'" (102)

3. "Maybe Guitar was right—partly. His life was pointless, aimless, and it was true that he didn't concern himself an awful lot about other people. There was nothing he wanted bad enough to risk anything for, inconvenience himself for." (107)

_____

_____

_____

_____

_____

_____

_____

4. "After a while he realized that nobody was walking on the other side of the street." (78)

_____

_____

_____

_____

_____

_____

_____

2. Student Model of Quotation Analysis

This excerpt includes a student thesis and a paragraph with evidence that proves the thesis. We have often found it helpful to give students only part of a model essay so that they can focus on recognizing and developing one skill at a time. Here, that skill is integrating quotations effectively and structuring a paragraph logically.

THESIS

The missionaries in Chinua Achebe's *Things Fall Apart* use rhetorical devices to attack the Ibo religion and the customs and traditions inherent to the religion. Achebe demonstrates the ability of rhetoric to indoctrinate the Ibo people into Christian values and Western laws, causing cultural destruction and chaos.

MODEL QUOTATION ANALYSIS

The following passage portrays Christianity as more appealing than the traditional religious beliefs of the Ibo people. The European missionaries preach not only through sermons, but also through hymns: "Then the missionaries burst into song. It was one of those gay and rollicking tunes of evangelism which had the power of plucking at silent and dusty chords in the heart of an Ibo man" (Achebe 146). Achebe notes the generic "Ibo man" to imply that the Christian hymns appeal to all types of people, not just to outcasts or those without rank or titles. Achebe calls attention to the particular power that song has over the Ibo people. The Ibo live in a society in which musical expression is almost as important as verbal expression. Achebe suggests the existence of a universal "desire" for soothing sounds while noting that that appreciation may not always surface to the human consciousness. Achebe further emphasizes this lack of consciousness with the phrase "dusty chords," suggesting that the appeal to soothing sounds is not invoked frequently. Achebe uses diction that suggests happiness when he says that the tune was "gay" and "rollicking," creating a relaxed and carefree tone. These calming, harmonious tunes contrast in various parts of the novel with the "frantic rhythm" (Achebe 50) of the drums typical of Ibo religious ceremonies. Achebe portrays an element of the presentation of Christianity that "strikes a chord" with the Ibo people, as the missionaries literally use music to manipulate their prospective converts. The psychological power play between the two cultures works to their advantage as the novelty of ideas (in this case, expressed through music) gives the missionaries power. Furthermore, Achebe emphasizes the power of hymns to suggest that the Ibo are not necessarily won over by the content of the missionaries' teachings but rather by its presentation: music merely acts as a vague tune of evangelism rather than as a coherent statement about

Christianity. It is the idea of a new faith that animates the Ibo, rather than a careful consideration of the pros and cons. As the novel progresses, the traditional Ibo drums disappear from the story as new Christian songs take their place, paralleling the decline of the Ibo culture.

3. Orwell Group Writing

"POLITICS AND THE ENGLISH LANGUAGE" BY GEORGE ORWELL

Review Orwell's definition of the following terms, then explain them in your own words and provide your own examples from the contemporary world.

1. *Dying metaphors*

   a. Explanation:

   b. Example(s):

2. *Operators,* **or** *verbal false limbs*

   a. Explanation:

   b. Examples:

3. *Pretentious diction*

   a. Explanation:

   b. Examples:

4. *Meaningless words*

   a. Explanation:

   b. Examples:

According to Orwell, what is the most disastrous cause and effect of using these four errors in writing?

With your group, rewrite the following sentences using Orwell's instructions on how *not* to write (i.e., write against his advice). Try to use as many of the above "techniques" as possible.

1. *Clear original:* Students in Senior English are expected to complete homework each night.

Revised: In an appeal to their learning about the basic humanity illustrated in classical literary works, students of International Baccalaureate Senior English are not discouraged from exhibiting a tendency toward completing work assigned to be addressed at their homes.

2. *Clear original:* The fog slowed my drive to school.

*Revised:*_____

_____

_____

_____

_____

_____

3. *Clear original:* I enjoy playing football.

*Revised:*_____

_____

_____

_____

_____

_____

4. *Clear original:* I find school lunches unappetizing.

*Revised:*_____

_____

_____

_____

_____

_____

4. Word Economy

Adapted from Doyle Online Writing Lab, http://academic.reed.edu/ writing/grammar_review/word_economy.html.

Try not to be too concerned with word economy when you're writing a first draft. Once you've finished writing, you can go back through your draft and review the sections that were the hardest to write. These sections probably include some "fillers"— unnecessary language that you can clean up or remove during your review. Combing through your writing and restructuring it into a more concise form can be challenging, but it makes your paper much easier to read.

1.   **Use active verbs whenever possible.**

Example 1:
She is appreciative of their efforts.

More concise:
She appreciates their efforts.

2.   **Often you can omit the word** *this* **from the beginning of a sentence. Try joining it to the last sentence with a comma.**

Example 2:
I was in an automobile accident when I was very young. This has resulted in my being an especially cautious driver.

More concise:
I was in an automobile accident when I was very young, and am consequently a very cautious driver.

3. *Could,* *should,* and *would* are overused terms. Replace them with strong verbs where appropriate.

    Example 3:
    The children could see that something was wrong.

    More concise:
    The children saw that something was wrong.

4. Quite often, words ending in *-tion* and *-sion* can be replaced by strong verbs.

    Example 4:
    He succeeded in the apprehension of the suspect.

    More concise:
    He apprehended the suspect.

5. The Beauty of Strong Verbs

Consult this list of verbs when seeking ways to articulate what a literary device reveals in a story, how an author creates a specific aspect of the story, how we might interpret an author's message, and so on. Add your own verbs to the list. These verbs will provide alternatives to dull "to be" verbs (*am, is, are, was, were, be, being, been*) and the literary essay constants *use* and *show*.*

Consider, for example, the differences among the following sentences. Which *contains* the strongest verb? How do verbs *alter* sentence structure?

First draft:
The symbol of the fire *gives off* an idea that Okonkwo is violent and destructive.

Second draft:
The symbol of the fire *is used to show* that Okonkwo is violent and destructive.

Third draft:
The symbol of the fire *illuminates* that Okonkwo is violent and destructive.

Fourth draft:
The symbol of the fire *illuminates* Okonkwo's violent, destructive nature.

Be careful not to avoid "to be" verbs if they are crucial to expressing your idea clearly. As you work to develop your writing voice, try to strike a balance between strong and passive verbs.

1. outline		21. provoke
2. illustrate		22. differentiate
3. describe		23. argue
4. depict		24. illuminate
5. evoke		25. emphasize
6. manipulate		26. interpret
7. entice		27. reveal
8. appeal		28. teach
9. suggest		29. compare
10. display		30. contrast
11. highlight		31. articulate
12. point out		32. demonstrate
13. criticize		33. idealize
14. praise		34.
15. villainize		35.
16. foreshadow		36.
17. anticipate		37.
18. reflect		38.
19. create		39.
20. delineate		40.

6. Peer Review Guidelines

Please follow these instructions to help your fellow writers strengthen their papers. Editors, please make specific suggestions both in discussion and in writing. Use this page for feedback on content, and mark copyediting suggestions on your partners' papers.

Writer's Name: Editor #1:

                                      Editor #2:

1. Read the first paragraph. STOP. Are you interested in continuing to read? Explain briefly why or why not. In your own words, tell what you think this essay will discuss.

2. Finish reading the essay, marking passages that seem vague or unclear to you, then tell the main point of the essay in your own words.

3. Are the opening and closing paragraphs accurate guides to the paper's focus? Explain why or why not.

_____

_____

_____

_____

_____

_____

4. What is the single strongest feature of the essay, the one thing that should not be lost in editing?

_____

_____

_____

_____

_____

_____

5. What unanswered questions remain in your mind when you've finished the essay?

_____

_____

_____

_____

_____

_____

6. For the moment, accept the writer's point of view. Try to extend the essay's argument by providing additional examples, by suggesting questions that might provoke further thought, and by discussing parallels.

_____
_____
_____
_____
_____
_____
_____

7. What objections might be raised against this argument? Provide counterevidence and counterarguments for the author. Are there other solutions or interpretations for this problem?

_____
_____
_____
_____
_____
_____
_____

8. Based on your experience as a writer, what suggestions might you give the writer of this paper?

_____
_____
_____
_____
_____
_____

APPENDIX F

1. Student Instructions for *Their Eyes Were Watching God* Pastiche

Name _____

Date _____

Period _____

A pastiche is a paper that mimics a writer's style without duplicating it. Your job is to create a paper that demonstrates your understanding and analysis of Hurston's style in an original form. The entire paper may not exceed 1,000 words.

As a way to explain your ideas, you will need to create a statement of intent. The statement acknowledges the author and text from which you created the pastiche; it identifies your chosen form for the creative assignment (pastiche), Hurston's stylistic elements you discuss, and how you explore those elements. The statement of intent should offer the reader a clear thesis and be well organized with specific support.

Following the statement of intent, the pastiche will be a two- to three-page vignette that imitates Hurston's poetic style and incorporates dialogue written in a nonstandard dialect. You may opt for Hurston's southern African American dialect or for another dialect that fits your story. It may be an additional scene related to *Eyes* or a scene/character that you create that mirrors a theme or character trait you analyzed.

Outline Due: _____   20 pts.   Evaluation:
Rough Draft Due: _____   25 pts.   A. Topic
Final Draft Due: _____   100 pts.   B. Knowledge
                                                      C. Organization
                                                      D. Language

Option 1:
- Choose a scene we hear about but don't witness firsthand or a scene you can imagine taking place based on what Hurston wrote.
- Make certain the scene has a beginning and ending.
- Make characterization and setting consistent with the novel.
- Use Hurston's narrative voice/poetic style to create a sense of place and a mood for the scene.
- Follow Hurston's patterns of dialect.

Option 2:

- Create an original setting and at least two developed characters for your vignette.
- Make certain the scene has a beginning and ending.
- Develop characterization, setting, and/or theme to mirror Hurston's purpose.
- Use Hurston's narrative voice/poetic style to create a sense of place and a mood for the scene.
- Include a list of ten rules for your dialect and clearly identify the type of dialect.

2. Final Grading Rubric for Character Conversations

	1-2 POINTS	3-4 POINTS	5-6 POINTS
WHAT ARE THEY READING IN THE CAFÉ?	No reading material mentioned.	Reading material is mentioned, but the reason why is unclear.	Reading materials and the reason for the choice is clear.

6 points possible for each character   _____/18 points total

	1-2 POINTS	3-4 POINTS	5-6 POINTS
HEROES	The individuals' definition of a hero or who they look up to is not mentioned or clear in the conversation.	A hero or important figure is mentioned correctly, but the traits or characteristics for why they are a hero are not included.	Who the individual looks up to as a hero is demonstrated, and reasons and actions the hero has committed are listed.

6 points possible for each character   _____/18 points total

	1-2 POINTS	3-4 POINTS	5-6 POINTS
TRUTH	Truth and how the three people define it are not mentioned.	The location and source of truth for the three are mentioned, but no reasons why are included.	The location and source of truth for the three are mentioned and historical or core values are included to tell why they believe the truth is there.

6 points possible for each character   _____/18 points total

	1-2 POINTS	3-4 POINTS	5-6 POINTS
CORE BELIEFS	No core beliefs or values are mentioned.	Core beliefs for each individual are mentioned, and they accurately reflect the beliefs of their literary movement.	Beliefs are mentioned, they are correct, and there are details about the historical reasons or sources for these core beliefs.

6 points possible for each character   _____/18 points total

	1–2 POINTS	3–4 POINTS	5–6 POINTS
ARGUMENT	An argument does not exist, or it exists but the subject of the argument is unclear.	An argument exists and there are a few details/reasons included about why they disagree.	There is a clear argument with lots of details describing why each individual possesses his or her own beliefs and does not agree with other people.

6 points total

3. Assignment for Trial of *Heart of Darkness*

HEART OF DARKNESS FINAL ASSESSMENT

or Deciphering Inscrutable Blackness: Trying Kurtz, Marlow, and Conrad

In the last few weeks, some of you have grown to enjoy Conrad's complex novella. Some of you have grown more and more frustrated with his lack of directness and long-winded narration. You now have a chance to turn those feelings of contentment and ire into an assessment. Together we will put Mr. Conrad on trial and decide if his novel should continue to be assigned widely in high schools across the world, or if the time has come to relegate him to the dustbin of progress. The assignment breaks into two components:

1. *Pretrial position statement:* **From your character's perspective, is** *Heart of Darkness* **a classic and worth reading? Why/why not? Attorneys can use half of this page to pose questions of the characters.**

    Evaluation: One page of writing, to be evaluated on conciseness of statement and skill in persuading the reader, using textual evidence

2. *Posttrial reflection:* **How have your ideas about** *Heart of Darkness* **been challenged? Have you changed your mind at all? Why or why not?**

    Evaluation: One page of writing, to be evaluated on conciseness of statement and skill in persuading the reader, using evidence from the trial
    Evaluation: Participation and performance (including T-chart tracking of arguments)

ROLES

Please choose three and list in order of preference (for assigning of roles):

*   **Chinua Achebe, defending his essay "An Image of Africa: Racism in Conrad's** *Heart of Darkness"*
*   **Joseph Conrad**
*   **Mr. Kurtz**
*   **Marlow**
*   **Narrator of** *Heart of Darkness* **(sailor on the** *Nellie***)**
*   **General manager**

- Kurtz's fiancé
- Team of three "modernist modernizers," who offer an alternative, updated version of the text
- Classics defenders (three) who offer reasons for reading the novel as it is
- Jury members (thirteen)
- Pair of defense attorneys, who call to the stand and question characters (maximum two questions per character) in defense of the story and the book
- Pair of prosecuting attorneys, who organize characters to critique the book (can cross-examine with a maximum of two questions per character)

See class calendar for dates for assigning roles, prep in class, and the trial.

4. Soundtrack Assignment

THE GREAT GATSBY SOUNDTRACK ASSIGNMENT

Have you ever wondered who picks out the music that plays in the background of a movie you are watching? That person is called a music supervisor. As you may know, *The Great Gatsby* is being made into a new movie, slated to hit theaters in 2012. It will be directed by Baz Lurhmann, a director known for his creative use of music in film.

YOUR TASK

Step 1: Imagine you are Baz Luhrmann's music supervisor. As we read *The Great Gatsby*, think about songs that would go well in certain scenes. Use the "Soundtrack Brainstorming" sheet in your folder to jot down your good ideas.
Step 2: Select five songs and connect them with five scenes in *The Great Gatsby*. Write out a playlist that includes the artist and song title and the page number(s) from the scene where the song will play.
Step 3: Write one paragraph for each song, explaining why that song connects to the scene you have chosen.

• **You must refer to** *symbols* **and** *themes* **that we have discussed in class. (Use your bookmarks as a reference.)**
• **Use quotes from the book to support the connection.**

This assignment is your final test on The Great Gatsby. You will have time to work on this assignment in class at least twice, but you may begin working any time.

Due date: _____

5. Soundtrack Brainstorming

Song(s):	Song(s):
Event and page number:	Event and page number:
Why did I choose this song?	Why did I choose this song?

6. Soundtrack Example

The Great Gatsby Soundtrack

SONG	SCENE
1. "I Don't Want to Get Over You" by The Magnetic Fields	Pp. 87–90 Jay Gatsby and Daisy Buchanan finally reunite.
2.	
3.	
4.	
5.	

1. When Daisy and Jay finally reunite on pages 87–90, my soundtrack will feature The Magnetic Fields' song "I Don't Want to Get Over You." Jay and Daisy, once young lovers, have every reason to move on. Daisy is now married with a little girl and a lavish home on East Egg. But, as the song says, Jay is unwilling to "leave this agony behind . . . and try to get you off my mind." Instead, he dedicates his life to amassing a fortune to impress and win back Daisy. All his hard work leads up to the moment when he invites Daisy over to see his home. The relationship between Jay and Daisy illustrates one of the book's central themes: unrequited love, and so does this Magnetic Fields song. Jay loves Daisy with a singularity that consumes him; after he finally sees Daisy again, Nick says that he "literally glowed; without a word or gesture

Beyond the Five-Paragraph Essay by Kimberly Hill Campbell and Kristi Latimer. Copyright © 2012. Stenhouse Publishers.

of exultation a new well-being radiated from him and filled the little room."
The song speaks to this type of devotion, saying, "I don't want to get over you
because I don't want to get over love."

7. Gatsby Soundtrack Assignment Rubric

Due date: _____

GREAT PAPER	IT'S OKAY	TRY AGAIN
Five songs and five scenes are selected and ordered correctly.	Five songs and five scenes are selected, with some mistakes in order.	Fewer than five songs and five scenes are selected, or there are major problems with ordering.
Meaningful connections between the songs and the scenes are made.	Connections between the songs and scenes are present, but weak.	Connections between songs and scenes are absent or confusing.
Several quotes from song lyrics and the novel are used to support connections.	Quotes are used, but done so sparingly or with little impact.	Quotes are not used, or are not used appropriately.
Meaningful and well-supported connections to both symbols and themes are present.	Connections to symbols and themes are present, but not in each paragraph, or with limited support.	Connections to symbols and themes are not made.

SUGGESTED WORKS

Following is a list of the works cited in the book as potential texts for students.

Achebe, Chinua. 1977. "An Image of Africa: Racism in Conrad's *Heart of Darkness*." *Massachusetts Review* 18: 782–794.

———. 1994. *Things Fall Apart*. New York: Anchor.

Albanese, Rory, and Jon Stewart, producers. *The Daily Show*. New York: Comedy Central.

Alexie, Sherman. 2007. *The Absolutely True Diary of a Part-Time Indian*. New York: Little, Brown.

Anderson, Laurie Halse. 1999. *Speak*. New York: Farrar, Straus and Giroux.

Angelou, Maya. 1969. *I Know Why the Caged Bird Sings*. New York: Random House.

Austen, Jane. 2003. *Pride and Prejudice*. New York: Barnes and Noble Classics.

———. 2004. *Sense and Sensibility*. New York: Barnes and Noble Classics.

Austen, Jane, and Nancy Butler. 2010. *Pride and Prejudice*. Illustrated by Hugo Petrus. New York: Marvel.

Bauer, Joan. 2001. "Letter from the Fringe." In *On the Fringe*, ed. Donald Gallo. New York: Dial.

Bernstein, Robert. 2003. "Theodor Seuss Geisel." In *Farewell, Godspeed: The Greatest Eulogies of Our Time*, ed. Cyrus M. Copeland. New York: Harmony Books.

Bradbury, Ray. 1953. *Fahrenheit 451*. New York: Del Ray.

———. 1983. *Something Wicked This Way Comes*. New York: Scribner.

———. 2003a. "Hunter of Metaphors." In *The Writing Life: Writers on How They Think and Write*, ed. Marie Arana. New York: Public Affairs.

———. 2003b. *The Best of Ray Bradbury: The Graphic Novel*. New York: IBooks.

Bradbury, Ray, and Tim Hamilton. 2009. *Ray Bradbury's Fahrenheit 451: The Authorized Adaptation*. New York: Farrar, Straus and Giroux.

Chopin, Kate. 2011. *The Awakening*. New York: Simon and Brown.

Cisneros, Sandra. 1991. *House on Mango Street*. New York: Vintage.

Collier, Eugenia. 1994. "Marigolds." In *Coming of Age in America: A Multicultural Anthology*, ed. Mary Frosch. New York: New Press.

Collins, Billy. 2001. "Sonnet." In *Sailing Around the Room: New and Selected Poems*. New York: Random House.

Collins, Suzanne. 2008. *The Hunger Games*. The Hunger Games series. New York: Scholastic.

————. 2009. *Catching Fire*. The Hunger Games series. New York: Scholastic.

————. 2010. *Mockingjay*. The Hunger Games series. New York: Scholastic.

Conrad, John Sr. 1997. "John Conrad Jr." In *The Book of Eulogies: A Collection of Memorial Tributes, Poetry, Essays, and Letters of Condolence*, ed. Phyllis Theroux. New York: Scribner.

Conrad, Joseph. 2010. *Heart of Darkness*. Madison, WI: Cricket House.

Crick, Mark. 2005. *Kafka's Soup: A Complete History of World Literature in 14 Recipes*. Orlando, FL: Harcourt.

Cronin, Doreen. 2000. *Click, Clack, Moo: Cows That Type*. New York: Simon and Schuster.

Crutcher, Chris. 1989. "The Pin." In *Athletic Shorts: Six Short Stories*, ed. Milton Crane. New York: Bantam Classics.

————. 2003. "Bawlbaby." In *King of the Mild Frontier: An Ill-Advised Autobiography*. New York: Greenwillow Books.

Cummings, E. E. 1956. "maggie and millie and molly and may." Poets.org. http://www.poets.org/viewmedia.php/prmMID/15406.

Cunningham, Michael. 2000. *The Hours*. New York: Picador.

Cushman, Kathleen, and the students of What Kids Can Do. 2003. *Fires in the Bathroom: Advice for Teachers from High School Students*. New York: The New Press.

Cushman, Kathleen, Laura Rogers, and the students of What Kids Can Do. 2008. *Fires in the Middle School Bathroom: Advice for Teachers from Middle Schoolers*. New York: The New Press.

Dahl, Roald. 1990. "The Way Up to Heaven." In *The Best of Roald Dahl*. New York: Vintage.

Dickinson, Emily. 2000. "Because I Could Not Stop for Death." In *Emily Dickinson's Poems*, ed. Johanna Brownell. Edison, NJ: Castle.

————. 2000. "This Is My Letter to the World." In *Emily Dickinson's Poems*, ed. Johanna Brownell. Edison, NJ: Castle.

————. 2002. *Emily Dickinson's Letters to the World*. New York: Farrar, Straus and Giroux.

Dickinson, Susan Gilbert. 1997. "Emily Dickinson." In *The Book of Eulogies: A Collection of Memorial Tributes, Poetry, Essays, and Letters of Condolence*, ed. Phyllis Theroux. New York: Scribner.

Dillard, Annie. 1987. *An American Childhood*. New York: Harper Perennial.

Dorris, Michael. 1987. *A Yellow Raft in Blue Water*. New York: Henry Holt.

Ellis, Deborah. 2000. *The Breadwinner*. Berkeley, CA: Publishers Group West.

Emerson, Ralph Waldo. 1997. "Henry David Thoreau." In *The Book of Eulogies: A Collection of Memorial Tributes, Poetry, Essays, and Letters of Condolence*, ed. Phyllis Theroux. New York: Scribner.

Erlich, Amy, ed. 1999. *When I Was Your Age, Volume Two: Original Stories About Growing Up*. Cambridge, MA: Candlewick.

Suggested Works

Fershleiser, Rachel, and Larry Smith, eds. 2008. *Not Quite What I Was Planning: Six-Word Memoirs by Writers Famous and Obscure*. New York: Harper Perennial.

Fitzgerald, F. Scott. 1995. *The Great Gatsby*. New York: Scribner.

———. 1998. "Winter Dreams." Board of Trustees of the University of South Carolina. http://www.sc.edu/fitzgerald/winterd/winter.html.

Frost, Robert. 1936. "Desert Places." American Poems. http://www.americanpoems.com/poets/robertfrost/691.

———. 1973a. "Stopping By Woods on a Snowy Evening." In *The Norton Anthology of Modern Poetry*, ed. Richard Ellman and Robert O'Clair. New York: Norton.

———. 1973b. "The Road Not Taken." In *The Norton Anthology of Modern Poetry*, ed. Richard Ellman and Robert O'Clair. New York: Norton.

Golding, William. 1959. *Lord of the Flies*. New York: Perigree Books.

Guisewite, Cathy. 2003. "Charles Schulz." In *Farewell, Godspeed: The Greatest Eulogies of Our Time*, ed. Cyrus M. Copeland. New York: Harmony Books.

Hawthorne, Nathaniel. 1981. *The Scarlet Letter*. New York: Bantam Classics.

Hill, Lister. 2003. "Helen Keller." In *Farewell, Godspeed: The Greatest Eulogies of Our Time*, ed. Cyrus M. Copeland. New York: Harmony Books.

Homer, and Ray Thomas. 2009. *The Odyssey*. Illustrated by Greg Tocchini. New York: Marvel.

Hughes, Langston. 2003. "Mother to Son." *In Teaching with Fire: Poetry That Sustains the Courage to Teach*, ed. Sam M. Intrator and Megan Scribner. San Francisco: Jossey-Bass.

———. 1959. "As I Grow Older." *In Selected Poems of Langston Hughes: A Classic Collection of Poems by a Master of American Verse*. New York: Vintage.

Hurst, James. 1960. "The Scarlet Ibis." http://209.184.141.5/westwood/academ/depts/dpteng/l-coker/virtualenglish/englsih%20i/english%20ia/scarlet_ibis.htm.

Hurston, Zora Neale. 2006. *Their Eyes Were Watching God*. New York: Harper Perennial Modern Classics.

Idle, Eric. 2003. "George Harrison." In *Farewell, Godspeed: The Greatest Eulogies of Our Time*, ed. Cyrus M. Copeland. New York: Harmony Books.

Ingersoll, Robert. 1997. "Walt Whitman." In *The Book of Eulogies: A Collection of Memorial Tributes, Poetry, Essays, and Letters of Condolence*, ed. Phyllis Theroux. New York: Scribner.

Isherwood, Christopher. 2003. "Virginia Woolf." In *Farewell, Godspeed: The Greatest Eulogies of Our Time*, ed. Cyrus M. Copeland. New York: Harmony Books.

Jackson, Shirley. 1948. "The Lottery." In *The Lottery and Other Stories*. New York: Noonday.

Johnson, Joel. 2011. "1 Million Workers. 90 Million iPhones. 17 Suicides. Who's to Blame?" *Wired*. http://www.wired.com/magazine/2011/02/ff_joelinchina/all/1.

Kennedy, Edward. 2003. "John F. Kennedy, Jr." In *Farewell, Godspeed: The Greatest Eulogies of Our Time*, ed. Cyrus M. Copeland. New York: Harmony Books.

Kidd, Sue Monk. 2001. *The Secret Life of Bees*. New York: Penguin.

Kimmel, Haven. 2001. *A Girl Named Zippy: Growing Up Small in Moreland, Indiana*. New York: Broadway.

Kingsolver, Barbara. 1992. *The Bean Trees*. New York: Harper.

Kingston, Maxine Hong. 1989. *The Woman Warrior: Memoirs of a Girlhood Among Ghosts*. New York: Vintage.

Knowles, John. 2003. *A Separate Peace*. New York: Scribner.

Krakauer, Jon. 2007. *Into the Wild*. New York: Anchor.

Lansky, Kathryn. 1998. *A Brilliant Streak: The Making of Mark Twain*. Orlando, FL: Harcourt Children's.

Lee, Harper. 2002 [1960]. *To Kill a Mockingbird*. New York: Harper Perennial Modern Classics.

Lesley, Craig. 1996. *Winter Kill*. New York: Picador.

London, Jack. 2006. "To Build a Fire." In *The Art of the Short Story: 52 Great Authors, Their Best Short Fiction, and Their Insights on Writing*, ed. Dana Gioia and R. S. Gwynn. New York: Pearson Longman.

Marquez, Gabriel Garcia. 1982. *Chronicle of a Death Foretold*. New York: Vintage.

May, Benjamin. 2003. "Martin Luther King." In *Farewell, Godspeed: The Greatest Eulogies of Our Time*, ed. Cyrus M. Copeland. New York: Harmony Books.

Mazer, Norma Fox. 1999. "In the Blink of an Eye." In *When I Was Your Age, Volume Two: Original Stories about Growing Up*, ed. Amy Erlich. Cambridge, MA: Candlewick.

McEwan, Ian. 2001. *Atonement*. New York: Anchor Books.

Meyer, Stephenie. 2005. *Twilight*. The Twilight Saga. New York: Little, Brown.

———. 2006. *New Moon*. The Twilight Saga. New York: Little, Brown.

———. 2007. *Eclipse*. The Twilight Saga. New York: Little, Brown.

———. 2008. *Breaking Dawn*. The Twilight Saga. New York: Little, Brown.

Miller, Arthur. 1996. *Death of a Salesman*. New York: Penguin.

———. 2003. *The Crucible*. New York: Penguin Classics.

Morrison, Toni. 2004. *Song of Solomon*. New York: Vintage.

Myers, Walter Dean. 2000. *145th Street: Short Stories*. New York: Dell Laurel-Leaf.

———. 2001. *Monster*. New York: HarperCollins.

Nelson, Blake. 2008. *Paranoid Park*. New York: Penguin.

New York Times. 1997. "Arthur Robert Ashe." In *The Book of Eulogies: A Collection of Memorial Tributes, Poetry, Essays, and Letters of Condolence*, ed. Phyllis Theroux. New York: Scribner.

Notaro, Laurie. 2002. "Extreme Clean Sports." In *The Idiot Girls Action-Adventure Club*. New York: Villard.

Nye, Naomi Shihab. 1997. *Sitti's Secret*. New York: Aladdin.

O'Connor, Flannery. 1971. "The Life You Save May Be Your Own." In *The Complete Stories of Flannery O'Connor*. New York: Farrar, Straus and Giroux.

Oliver, Mary. 1992. "Poppies." In *New and Selected Poems, Volume One*. Boston: Beacon.

Olsen, Tilie. 1995. "I Stand Here Ironing." In *Points of View: An Anthology of Short Stories*. Rev. ed. Edited by James Moffett and Kenneth McElheny. New York: Mentor.

Orwell, George. 1946. "Politics and the English Language." http://orwell.ru/library/essays/ politics/english/e_polit.

———. 1996. *Animal Farm*. New York: Signet.

———. 2008. "A Hanging," "Marrakech," "Revenge Is Sour," and "Shooting an Elephant." In *Facing Unpleasant Facts: Narrative Essays*, ed. George Packer. Orlando, FL: Harcourt.

Piercy, Marge. 2001. "Life of Prose and Poetry: An Inspiring Combination." In *Writers on Writing: Collected Essays from The New York Times*. New York: Times Books.

Plath, Sylvia. 1956. "The Queen's Complaint." American Poems. http://www.americanpoems. com/poets/sylviaplath/1448.

———. 1960. "Morning Song." Poets. http://www.poets.org/viewmedia.php/prmMID/15293.

Poe, Edgar Allan. 1984a. "The Black Cat." In *The Complete Stories and Poems of Edgar Allan Poe*. New York: Doubleday.

———. 1984b. "The Fall of the House of Usher" and "The Raven." In *The Complete Stories and Poems of Edgar Allan Poe*. New York: Doubleday.

Poe, Edgar Allan, and Gris Grimly. 2004. *Edgar Allan Poe's Tales of Mystery and Madness*. New York: Antheneum.

Poe, Edgar Allan, and Marcel DeJong. 2004. *Graphic Classics: Edgar Allan Poe*. 4th ed. Mt. Horeb, WI: Eureka.

Quindlen, Anna. 1993. "Mr. Smith Goes to Heaven." In *Thinking Out Loud: On the Personal, the Political, the Public, and the Private*. New York: Random House.

Quinlan, Sean. 1997. "John Fitzgerald Kennedy." In *The Book of Eulogies: A Collection of Memorial Tributes, Poetry, Essays, and Letters of Condolence*, ed. Phyllis Theroux. New York: Scribner.

Rylant, Cynthia. 1990. "Checkouts." In *A Couple of Kooks and Other Stories About Love*. New York: Orchard Books.

Salinger, J. D. 2001. *The Catcher in the Rye*. New York: Back Bay Books.

Satrapi, Marjane. 2003. *Persepolis*. New York: Pantheon.

Sawyer, Diane. 2003. "Lucille Ball." In *Farewell, Godspeed: The Greatest Eulogies of Our Time*, ed. Cyrus M. Copeland. New York: Harmony Books.

Schlosser, Eric. 2005. *Fast Food Nation*. New York: Harper Perennial.

Schmelling, Sarah. 2009. *Ophelia Joined the Group Maidens Who Don't Float: Classic Lit Signs on to Facebook*. New York: Plume.

Scieszka, Jon. 1996. *The True Story of the Three Little Pigs!* New York: Puffin.

Sedaris, David. 1997. *Naked*. New York: Back Bay Books/Little, Brown.

Seuss, Dr. 1971. *The Lorax*. New York: Random House.

Shakespeare, William. 1997. *Hamlet*. New York: Wordsworth Edition.

Shakespeare, William, and John McDonald. 2009. *"Romeo and Juliet" Original Text: Graphic Novel*. Litchborough, Towcester, UK: Classic Comics.

Sophocles. 1991. *Antigone*. In *Sophocles I*, ed. and trans. David Grene and Richmond Lattimore. Chicago: University of Chicago Press.

Soto, Gary. 1992. "Being Mean." In *Living Up the Street: Narrative Reflections*. New York: Bantam Doubleday Dell.

Smith, Kevin. 2007. *My Boring-Ass Life: The Uncomfortably Candid Diary of Kevin Smith*. London: Titan.

Spiegelman, Art. 1986. *Maus I: A Survivor's Tale: My Father Bleeds History*. New York: Pantheon.

Stafford, Kim. 1997. "William Stafford." In *The Book of Eulogies: A Collection of Memorial Tributes, Poetry, Essays, and Letters of Condolence*, ed. Phyllis Theroux. New York: Scribner.

Steinbeck, John. 1993. *Of Mice and Men*. New York: Penguin.

———. 2006. *Grapes of Wrath*. New York: Penguin Classics.

Stevens, Wallace. 1954. "Thirteen Ways of Looking at a Blackbird." Poetry Foundation. http://www.poetryfoundation.org/poem/174503.

Stevenson, Adlai Ewing. 1997. "Eleanor Roosevelt." In *The Book of Eulogies: A Collection of Memorial Tributes, Poetry, Essays, and Letters of Condolence*, ed. Phyllis Theroux. New York: Scribner.

Stewart, Jon, Ben Karlin, and Stephen Colbert, producers. *The Colbert Report*. New York: Comedy Central.

Stoppard, Tom. 1994. *Rosencrantz and Guildenstern Are Dead*. New York: Grove Press.

Tan, Amy. 1991. "Mother Tongue." In *The Best American Essays of the Century*, ed. Joyce Carol Oates. Boston: Houghton Mifflin.

Theroux, Phyllis, ed. 1997. *The Book of Eulogies: A Collection of Memorial Tributes, Poetry, Essays, and Letters of Condolence*. New York: Scribner.

Thoreau, Henry David. [1854]. 1995. *Walden*. New ed. New York: Houghton Mifflin.

Thoreau, Henry David, and Steven Schnur, ed. 2002. *Henry David's House*. New York: Charlesbridge.

Thurber, James. 1952. "The Catbird Seat." In *Fifty Great Short Stories*, ed. Milton Crane. New York: Bantam Classic.

Twain, Mark. [1885]. 1998. *Adventures of Huckleberry Finn*. 3rd ed. New York: W. W. Norton.

———. 2000. "Corn-Pone Opinions." In *The Best American Essays of the Century*, ed. Joyce Carol Oates. Boston: Houghton Mifflin.

Twain, Mark, Rick Geary, Evert Geradts, and Skip Williams. 2004. *Graphic Classics: Mark Twain*. Mt. Horeb, WI: Eureka Productions.

Updike, John. 2004. "Man and Daughter in the Cold." In *The Early Stories: 1953–1975*. New York: Ballantine.

Van Dyke, Henry. 2003. "Mark Twain. In *Farewell, Godspeed: The Greatest Eulogies of Our Time*, ed. Cyrus M. Copeland. New York: Harmony Books.

Vonnegut, Kurt. 1998. "Harrison Bergeron." In *Welcome to the Monkey House*. New York: Dial.

Walker, Alice. 2003. "Everyday Use." In *Love and Trouble: Stories of Black Women*. New York: Harvest.

Welty, Eudora. 1982. "A Worn Path." In *The New Collected Stories of Eudora Welty*. New York: Harvest Books.

Werlin, Nancy. 2001. "Shortcut." In *On the Fringe*, ed. Donald Gallo. New York: Speak.

White, E. B. 1997. "Daisy." In *The Book of Eulogies: A Collection of Memorial Tributes, Poetry, Essays, and Letters of Condolence*, ed. Phyllis Theroux. New York: Scribner.

Whitman, Walt. 1959. "Song of Myself, Part 1." In *Complete Poetry and Prose by Walt Whitman*, ed. James Miller Jr. Boston: Houghton Mifflin.

Willems, Mo. 2009. *Naked Mole Rat Gets Dressed*. New York: Hyperion Books for Children.

Williams, William Carlos. 1991. "The Red Wheelbarrow" and "This Is Just to Say." In *The Collected Poems of William Carlos Williams, Vol. 1, 1909–1939*, ed. A. Walton Litz and Christopher MacGowan. New York: New Directions.

Wolff, Tobias. 1997. "Bullet in the Brain." In *Night in Question: Stories*. New York: Vintage.

Woolf, Virginia. 1989. "The Mark on the Wall." In *The Complete Shorter Fiction of Virginia Woolf*. 2nd ed. New York: Harvest.

Wright, Richard. 1937. *Black Boy: A Record of Childhood and Youth*. New York: Harper and Brothers.

Write Source. http://www.thewritesource.com.

Yolen, Jane. 1992. *Letting Swift River Go*. Boston: Little, Brown.

———. 1999. "The Long Closet." In *When I Was Your Age, Volume Two: Original Stories About Growing Up*, ed. Amy Erlich. Cambridge, MA: Candlewick.

REFERENCES

Adelman, Clifford. 1999. "Why Can't We Stop Talking About the SAT?" *The Chronicle of Higher Education* 46 (11): 84–85.

Albertson, Bonnie R. 2007. "Organization and Development Features of Grade 8 and Grade 10 Writers: A Descriptive Study of Delaware Student Testing Program (DTSP) Essays." *Research in the Teaching of English* 41(4): 453–464.

Allen, Janet. 1995. *It's Never Too Late: Leading Adolescents to Lifelong Literacy.* Portsmouth, NH: Heinemann.

———. 1999. *Words, Words, Words: Teaching Vocabulary in Grades 4–12.* Portland, ME: Stenhouse.

———. 2007. "Mastering the Art of Effective Vocabulary Instruction." In *Adolescent Literacy: Turning Promise into Practice*, ed. Kylene Beers, Robert E. Probst, and Linda Rief. Portsmouth, NH: Heinemann.

Appleman, Deborah. 2007. "Interlude 3: Lessons Learned: Reading with Adolescents." In *Adolescent Literacy: Turning Promise into Practice*, ed. Kylene Beers, Robert E. Probst, and Linda Rief. Portsmouth, NH: Heinemann.

Argys, Richard. 2008. "One More Thing: Can We Teach Process and Formulaic Response?" *English Journal* 97(3): 97–101.

Atwell, Nancie. 1998. *In the Middle.* 2nd ed. Portsmouth, NH: Boynton/Cook.

Ballinger, Philip. 2008. "College Admissions Tests: Destructive Icons or Useful Tools?" *Teachers College Record.* http://www.tcrecord.org/content.asp?contentid=15431.

Blau, Sheridan. 2003. *The Literature Workshop: Teaching Texts and Their Readers.* Portsmouth, NH: Heinemann.

Booth, Wayne. 1988. *The Company We Keep: An Ethics of Fiction.* Berkeley: University of California Press.

Brannon, Lil, Jennifer Pooler Courtney, Cynthia P. Urbanski, Shana V. Woodward, Jeanie Marklin Reynolds, Anthony E. Iannone, Karen D. Haag, Karen Mach, Lacy Arnold Manship, and Mary Kendrick. 2008. "The Five-Paragraph Essay and the Deficit Model of Education." *English Journal* 98(2): 16–21.

Burke, Jim. 2000. *Reading Reminders: Tools, Tips, and Technology.* Portsmouth, NH: Boynton/Cook.

———. 2003. *The English Teacher's Companion.* 2nd ed. Portsmouth, NH: Heinemann.

Campbell, Kimberly. 2007. *Less Is More: Teaching Literature with Short Texts, Grades 6–12.* Portland, ME: Stenhouse.

Carlson, Erin. 2011. "*The House on Mango Street* Lesson Plan." OUSD Urban Dreams. http://urbandreams.ousd.k12.ca.us/lessonplans/mango_street2/index.htm.

Christenbury, Leila. 2006. *Making the Journey: Becoming a Teacher of English Language Arts.* 3rd ed. Portsmouth, NH: Heinemann.

Christenbury, Leila, and Patricia P. Kelly. 1993. *Questioning: A Path to Critical Thinking.* Urbana, IL: National Council of Teachers of English.

Christensen, Linda. 2000. *Reading, Writing, and Rising Up: Teaching About Social Justice and the Power of the Written Word.* Milwaukee, WI: Rethinking Schools.

———. 2009. *Teaching for Joy and Justice: Re-Imagining the Language Arts Classroom.* Milwaukee, WI: Rethinking Schools.

Courtney, Jennifer P. 2008. "Performing Student, Teacher, and Tutor of Writing: Negotiating Ideas of Writing in First-Year Writing Courses and Writing Center Tutorials." PhD diss. Charlotte: U of North Carolina.

Cushman, Kathleen, and the students of What Kids Can Do. 2003. *Fires in the Bathroom: Advice for Teachers from High School Students.* New York: The New Press.

Cushman, Kathleen, Laura Rogers, and the students of What Kids Can Do. 2008. *Fires in the Middle School Bathroom: Advice for Teachers from Middle Schoolers.* New York: The New Press.

Daniels, Harvey. 2002. *Literature Circles: Voice and Choice in Book Clubs and Reading Groups.* 2nd ed. Portland, ME: Stenhouse.

Daniels, Harvey, and Nancy Steineke. 2004. *Mini-Lessons for Literature Circles.* Portsmouth, NH: Heinemann.

Dunning, Stephen, and William Stafford. 1992. *Getting the Knack: 20 Poetry Exercises 20.* Urbana, IL: National Council of Teachers of English.

Dyer, Richard. 2007. *Pastiche.* New York: Routledge.

Eikmeier, Ginger M. 2008. "D'oh! Using the Simpsons to Improve Student Response in Literature." *English Journal* 97(4): 77–80.

Elbow, Peter. 1997. "High Stakes and Low Stakes in Assigning and Responding to Writing." In *Writing to Learn: Assigning and Responding to Writing Across the Disciplines*, ed. Mary Deane Sorcinelli and Peter Elbow. Vol. 69. San Francisco: Jossey-Bass.

Elbow, Peter, and Pat Belanoff. 2000. *Sharing and Responding.* 3rd ed. Columbus, OH: McGraw-Hill.

Fanetti, Susan, Kathy M. Bushrow, and David L. DeWeese. 2010. "Closing the Gap Between High School Writing Instruction and College Writing Expectations." *English Journal* 99(4): 77–83.

Fischer, Elizabeth A. 2000. "Prescriptions for Curing English Teacher Split Personality Disorder." *English Journal* 89(4): 40–45.

Fisher, Douglas, and Nancy Frey. 2003. "Writing Instruction for Struggling and Adolescent Readers: A Gradual Release Model." *The Journal of Adolescent and Adult Literacy* 46(5): 396–405.

Fletcher, Ralph. 1993. *What a Writer Needs.* Portsmouth, NH: Heinemann.

Flynn, Nick, and Shirley McPhillips. 2000. *A Note Slipped Under the Door: Teaching from Poems We Love.* Portland, ME: Stenhouse.

Gillespie, Tim. 1994. "Why Literature Matters." *English Journal* 83(8): 16–21

Goldberg, Natalie. 1990. "The Rules of Writing Practice." In *Wild Mind: Living the Writer's Life*. New York: Bantam Books.

Graham, Steve, and Dolores Perin. 2007. *Writing Next: Effective Strategies to Improve Writing of Adolescents in Middle and High Schools*. New York: Carnegie Corporation.

Green, Joey. 2011. *Selling Out: If Famous Authors Wrote Advertising*. Los Angeles: Lunatic.

Gross, Jane. 2003. "Sarah Lawrence College Drops SAT Requirement, Saying a New Writing Test Misses the Point." *The New York Times*. http://www.nytimes.com/2003/11/13/ nyregion/sarah-lawrence-college-drops-sat-requirement-saying-new-writing-test-misses .html.

Hipple, T. 2000. "With Themes for All: The Universality of the Young Adult Novel." In *Reading Their World: The Young Adult Novel in the Classroom*, ed. V. R. Monseau and G. M. Salvner. Portsmouth, NH: Heinemann.

International Baccalaureate Organization (IBO). 2002. Diploma requirements. http://www .haef.gr/gr/pcl/ib/english-a2.pdf.

International Reading Association/National Council of Teachers of English (IRA/NCTE). 1996. *Standards for the English Language Arts*. http://www.ncte.org/standards/ncte-ira. Newark, DE: International Reading Association and Urbana, IL: National Council of Teachers of English.

Jago, Carol. 2009. "Crash! The Currency Crisis in American Culture." A Report from the National Council of Teachers of English. Urbana, IL: National Council of Teachers of English.

Johannessen, Larry, Elizabeth Kahn, and Carolyn Calhoun Walter. 2009. *Writing About Literature*. 2nd ed. Urbana, IL: National Council of Teachers of English.

Kajder, Sara B. 2007. "Unleashing Potential with Emerging Technologies." In *Adolescent Literacy: Turning Promise into Practice*, ed. Kylene Beers, Robert E. Probst, and Linda Rief. Portsmouth, NH: Heinemann.

Kane, Loretta Sue. 2005. "A Developmental Approach to Investigating Differences in the Way High School Students of Varying Performance Levels Conceptualize Academic Essay Writing." PhD diss. Berkeley: University of California.

Keene, Ellin Oliver. 2007. "The Essence of Understanding." In *Adolescent Literacy: Turning Promise into Practice*, ed. Kylene Beers, Robert E. Probst, and Linda Rief. Portsmouth, NH: Heinemann.

Kidwell, Kirk S. 2005. "Understanding the College First-Year Experience." *The Clearing House* 78(6): 253–255.

Kittle, Penny. 2008. *Write Beside Them: Risk, Voice, and Clarity in High School Writing*. Portsmouth, NH: Heinemann.

Knoblauch, Cy, and Lil Brannon. 1984. *Rhetorical Traditions and the Teaching of Writing*. Upper Montclair, NJ: Boynton Cook.

References

Kramer, Stephen. 2005. "From a Writer's Notebook: No Training Wheels." In *The 9 Rights of Every Writer: A Guide for Teachers*, ed. Vicki Spandel. Portsmouth, NH: Heinemann.

Langer, Judith. 1992. "Rethinking Literature Instruction." In *Literature Instruction: A Focus on Student Response*. Urbana, IL: National Council of Teachers of English.

Lattimer, Heather. 2003. *Thinking Through Genre: Units of Study in Reading and Writing Workshops, 4–12*. Portland, ME: Stenhouse.

McHaney, Pearl Amelia. 2004. "Let Every Voice Be Heard: Focus Essays Create Democratic Classrooms." *English Journal* 93(5): 72–76.

Meyers, G. Douglas. 2002. "Whose Inquiry Is It Anyway? Using Students' Questions in the Teaching of Literature." In *Inquiry and the Literacy Text: Constructing Discussion in the English Classroom*, ed. James Holden and John Schmit. Urbana, IL: National Council of Teachers of English.

Miller, Jeanetta. 2010. "Persistence of the Five-Paragraph Essay." *English Journal* 93(3): 99–101.

Moffett, James. 1983. "On Essaying." In *Forum: Essays on Theory and Practice in the Teaching of Writing*, ed. Patricia L. Stock. Upper Montclair, NJ: Boynton/Cook.

Moghtader, Michael, Alanna Cotch, and Kristen Hague. 2001. "The First-Year Composition Requirement Revisited: A Survey." *College Composition and Communication* 52(3): 455–467.

Moss, Glenda. 2002. "The Five-Paragraph Theme: Does It Prepare Students for College?" *The Quarterly* 24(3): 23–25, 38.

Murray, Donald. 2007. "Teach Writing Your Way." In *Adolescent Literacy: Turning Promise into Practice*, ed. Kylene Beers, Robert E. Probst, and Linda Rief. Portsmouth, NH: Heinemann.

National Center for the Study of Writing and Literacy. 2011. Occasional Papers and Technical Reports. National Writing Project. http://www.nwp.org/cs/public/print/doc/resources/techreports.csp.

National Commission on Writing in America's Schools and Colleges. 2003. *The Neglected "R": The Need for a Writing Revolution*. The College Board. http://www.collegeboard.com/prod_downloads/writingcom/neglectedr.pdf.

National Council of Teachers of English (NCTE). 2004. *NCTE Beliefs About the Teaching of Writing*. http://www.ncte.org/about/over/positions/category/write/118876.htm.

Newkirk, Thomas. 2012. *The Art of Slow Reading*. Portsmouth, NH: Heinemann.

O'Brien, Peggy, ed. 1993. *Shakespeare Set Free: Teaching Romeo and Juliet, Macbeth, and A Midsummer Night's Dream*. New York: Washington Square Press.

O'Neill, Caroline. 2006. "Readers' Response Journal General Guidelines." International Baccalaureate English Summer Workshops. New York: United Nations International School.

Orlean, Susan, ed. 2005. "Introduction." In *The Best American Essays: 2005*. Boston: Houghton Mifflin.

Pearson, P. David, L. H. Roehler, J. A. Dole, and G. C. Duffy. 1992. "Developing Expertise in Reading Comprehension." In *What Research Has to Say About Reading Instruction*, ed. J. Samuels and A. Farstrup. Newark, DE: International Reading Association.

Postman, Neil. 1995. *The End of Education: Redefining the Value of School.* New York: Knopf.

Probst, Robert E. 2004. *Response & Analysis: Teaching Literature in Secondary School.* Portsmouth, NH: Heinemann.

———. 2007. "Tom Sawyer, Teaching, and Talking." In *Adolescent Literacy: Turning Promise into Practice*, ed. Kylene Beers, Robert E. Probst, and Linda Rief. Portsmouth, NH: Heinemann.

Prose, Francine. 2006. *Reading Like a Writer: A Guide for People Who Love Books and for Those Who Want to Write Them.* New York: Harper Perennial.

Purves, Alan C., Theresa Rogers, and Anna O. Soter. 1995. *How Porcupines Make Love III: Readers, Texts, Cultures in the Response-Based Literature Classroom.* White Plains, NY: Longman.

Randsell, D. R., and Gregory R. Glau. 1996. "Articulation and Student Voices: Eliminating the Perception That 'High School English Doesn't Teach Nothing.'" *English Journal* 85(1): 17–21.

Rideout, Victoria, J., Ulla L. Foehr, and Donald. F. Roberts. 2010. "Generation M2: Media in the Lives of 8–18-Year-Olds." Kaiser Family Foundation. http://www.kff.org/entmedia/upload/8010.pdf.

Rief, Linda. 1992. *Seeking Diversity: Language Arts with Adolescents.* Portsmouth, NH: Heinemann.

———. 2007. "Writing: Commonsense Matters." In *Adolescent Literacy: Turning Promise into Practice*, ed. Kylene Beers, Robert E. Probst, and Linda Rief. Portsmouth, NH: Heinemann.

Roessing, Lesley. 2004. "Toppling the Idol." *English Journal* 94(1): 41–46.

Romano, Tom. 1987. *Clearing the Way: Working with Teenage Writers.* Portsmouth, NH: Heinemann.

———. 2000. "The Living Legacy of Donald Murray." *English Journal* 89(3): 74–79.

———. 2004. *Crafting Authentic Voice.* Portsmouth, NH: Heinemann.

———. 2007. "Teaching Writing from the Inside." In *Adolescent Literacy: Turning Promise into Practice*, ed. Kylene Beers, Robert E. Probst, and Linda Rief. Portsmouth, NH: Heinemann.

Rorschach, Elizabeth. 2004. "The Five Paragraph Theme Redux." *The Quarterly* 26 (1): 17–19, and 25.

Rosenblatt, Louise M. 1978. *The Reader, the Text, the Poem: The Transactional Theory of the Literary Work.* Carbondale: Southern Illinois University Press.

———. 1995. "Continuing the Conversation: A Clarification." *Research in the Teaching of English* 29(October): 349–354.

Rosenblatt, Roger. 2011. *Unless It Moves the Human Heart: The Craft and Art of Writing*. New York: HarperCollins.

Scholes, Robert E. 1982. *Semiotics and Interpretation*. New Haven, CT: Yale University Press.

———. 1985. *Textual Power: Literary Theory and the Teaching of English*. New Haven, CT: Yale University Press.

Setoodeh, Ramin. 2005. "SAT: What's Your Score." *Newsweek*, April 4.

Smith, Mary Ann. 2005. "Are You Ready for College Writing?" *The Voice* 10(3): 1–2.

Sorcinelli, Mary Deane, and Peter Elbow, eds. 1997. *Writing to Learn: Assigning and Responding to Writing Across the Disciplines. New Directions for Teaching and Learning*. Vol. 69. San Francisco: Jossey-Bass.

Spandel, Vicki. 2005. *The 9 Rights of Every Writer: A Guide for Teachers*. Portsmouth, NH: Heinemann.

Strunk, William, and E. B. White. 2007. *The Elements of Style Illustrated*. Illus. Maira Kalman. New York: Penguin.

Tomlinson, Carol Ann. 1999. *The Differentiated Classroom: Responding to the Needs of All Learners*. Alexandria, VA: Association for Supervision and Curriculum Development.

Tomlinson, Carol Ann, and Jay McTighe. 2006. *Integrating Differentiated Instruction and Understanding by Design: Connecting Content and Kids*. Alexandria, VA: Association for Supervision and Curriculum Development.

Tovani, Cris. 2000. *I Read It, but I Don't Get It: Comprehension Strategies for Adolescent Readers*. Portland, ME: Stenhouse.

———. 2004. *Do I Really Have to Teach Reading? Content Comprehension, Grades 6–12*. Portland, ME: Stenhouse.

Ueland, Brenda. [1938]. 1987. *If You Want to Write: A Book About Art, Independence, and Spirit*. 2nd ed. St. Paul, MN: Graywolf.

Vygotsky, Lev. 1962. *Thought and Language*. Ed. and trans. Eugenia Hanfman and Gertrude Vakar. Cambridge, MA: MIT Press.

———. 1978. *Mind in Society: The Development of Higher Psychological Processes*. Edited by Michael Cole, Vera John-Steiner, Sylvia Scribner, and Ellen Souberman. Cambridge, MA: Harvard University Press.

Webb, Don. 2006. "The Critics Corner: Writing Pastiches." Bewildering Stories. http://www.bewilderingstories.com/ issue197/cc_pastiche.html.

Wesley, Kimberly. 2000. "The Ill Effects of the Five Paragraph Theme." *English Journal* 90(1): 57–60.

Wiggins, Grant, and Jay McTighe. 1998. *Understanding by Design*. Alexandria, VA: Association for Supervision and Curriculum Development.

———. 2005. *Understanding by Design*. 2nd ed. Alexandria, VA: Association for Supervision and Curriculum Development.

Wiley, Mark. 2000. "The Popularity of Formulaic Writing (and Why We Need to Resist)." *English Journal* 90(1): 61–67.

Zinsser, William, ed. 1998. *Inventing the Truth: The Art and Craft of Memoir*. Boston: Houghton Mifflin.

INDEX